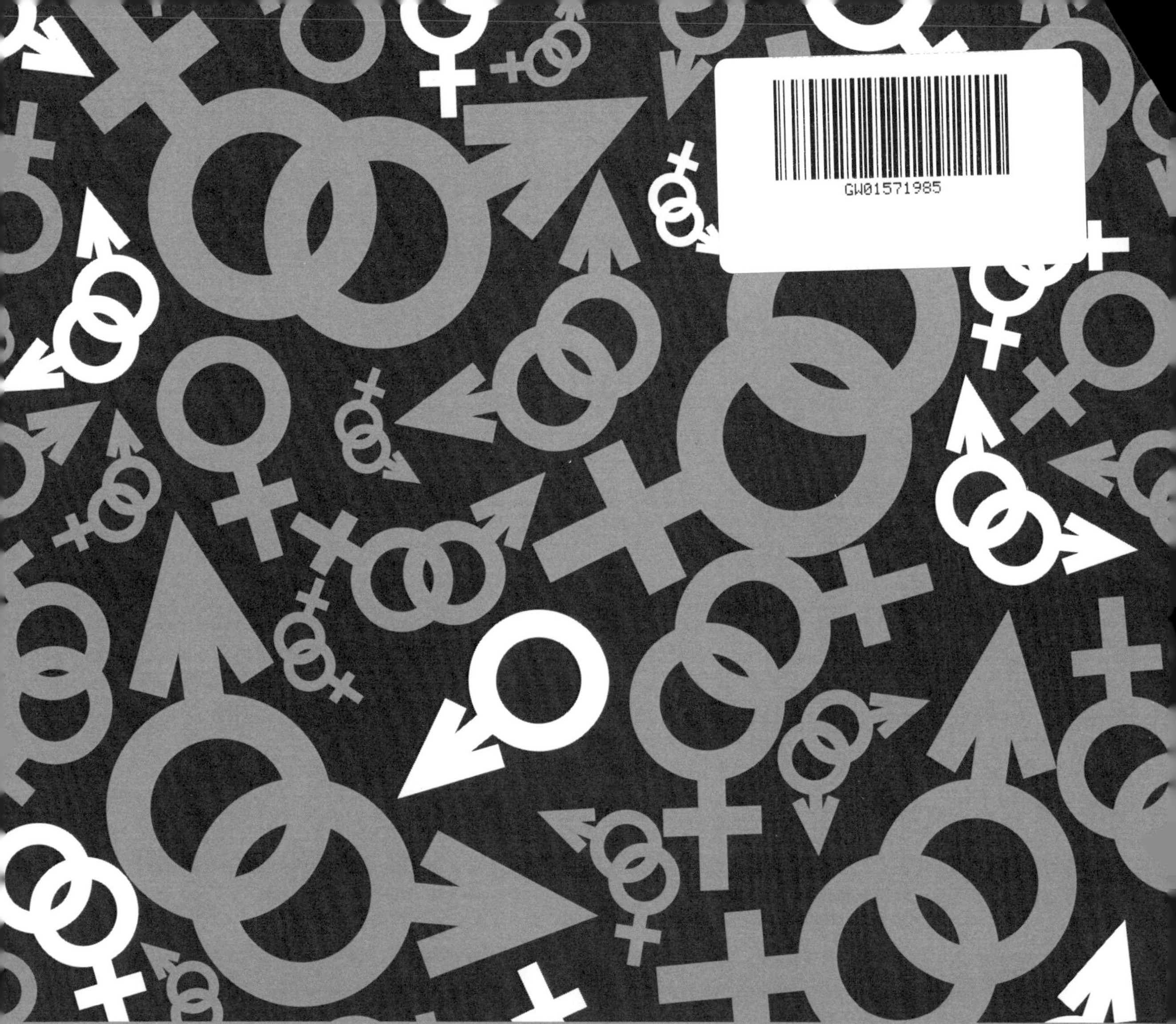

Sexuality and Learning Disabilities

A handbook

Edited by Michelle McCarthy and David Thompson
Foreword by Hilary Brown

Sexuality and Learning Disabilities
A handbook

© Pavilion Publishing (Brighton) Ltd 2010

The authors have asserted their rights in accordance with the Copyright, Designs and Patents Act 1988 to be identified as the authors of this work.

Published by:
Pavilion Publishing (Brighton) Ltd – part of OLM Group
Richmond House
Richmond Road
Brighton
BN2 3RL
UK

Tel: 01273 623222
Fax: 01273 625556
Email: info@pavpub.com
Web: www.pavpub.com

First published 2010

All rights reserved. No part of this publication may be copied without fee or prior permission by the purchaser subject to both of the following conditions: that the item is reproduced in its entirety, including the copyright acknowledgement; that the copies are used solely by the person or organisation purchasing the original publication.

A Catalogue reference for this book is available from the British Library.

ISBN: 978 1 84196 286 3

Pavilion is the leading training and development provider and publisher in the health, social care and allied fields, providing a range of innovative training solutions underpinned by sound research and professional values. We aim to put our customers first, through excellent customer service and good value.

Editor: Sanaz Nazemi, Pavilion
Cover design: Emma Garbutt, Pavilion
Illustrations: Katie Scott
Page layout and typesetting: Anthony Pitt, Pavilion
Printed on paper from a sustainable resource by: Ashford Press

Contents

Acknowledgements 2

Foreword 3

Contributors 9

Introduction 13

Chapter 1: People with learning disabilities, sex and the law 25
Claire Fanstone and David Thompson

Chapter 2: Masturbation 41
Paul Cambridge

Chapter 3: Menstruation and menopause 53
Michelle McCarthy

Chapter 4: Sexuality support for people with profound and multiple disabilities 65
Angela Mallett and David Stewart

Chapter 5: Sexual interests, opportunities and choices 81
David Thompson

Chapter 6: Supporting relationships – lessons from what people with learning disabilities have to say 97
Joan Lesseliers, Geert Van Hove and Tom Van Hoey

Chapter 7: Pregnancy, contraception and women choosing to have a child 109
Sandra Baum and Natasha Alexander

Chapter 8: Concerns about people with learning disabilities being sexually abused 125
Deborah Kitson

Chapter 9: Unacceptable sexual behaviour 141
David Thompson

Chapter 10: Sex education with individuals and in groups 157
Seema Fitzwater and Jane Noonan

Acknowledgements

The editors would like to thank all the authors for their contributions to this book and Hilary Brown for writing the foreword. We would also like to thank Sanaz Nazemi and Jan Alcoe from Pavilion Publishing for their advice at various stages of this project and to Pavilion more generally for their long-standing commitment to publish work in this area. As always, the editors are most grateful to all the people with learning disabilities they have worked with over the many years and for sharing their experiences.

Michelle McCarthy and David Thompson

Foreword

It is a privilege to have been asked to write the foreword for this helpful and respectful book. Sexuality in learning disability services has always been seen as a 'problem' but here there are suggestions about making it a positive in people's lives.

There is a long and a short history to these issues. The last 150 years have seen a sea of change in the understanding of and provision for people with intellectual disabilities in our families, schools and communities. Throughout that time, sexuality has been a critical issue often acting as a litmus test of public acceptance. Traditional services bounced men and women with learning disabilities back and forth between being seen as sexless innocents or as degenerate monsters (Brown, 1994). Because they were often living under the gaze of others, their sexuality was often judged by those who were motivated to keep a veil of false respectability over the realities of sex.

But since the 1980s there has been a very clear commitment to enabling and respecting people with learning disabilities and increasing their sexual options. Starting with Ann Craft's pioneering work (1978; 1987; 1994) and continuing with Michelle McCarthy and David Thompson's writing, this commitment has been expressed through targeted sex education (McCarthy, 2003) through one-to-one counselling and support, through a more honest appraisal of when relationships are unwanted or abusive (Brown & Turk, 1992; McCarthy, 2003) and through significant changes in the law which recognise that people with learning disabilities are entitled to enter into relationships on the same terms as others, unless these are exploitative or occur in the absence of valid consent (Fanstone, 2005).

Where once learning disability was used as a rationale for labelling people, for locking them away and for shutting them up, it is now often assumed that people will fend for themselves and deal with powerful emotions and practical difficulties with minimal support. We have moved from the vast congregate settings of the large asylums to the aspiration for personalised, tailor-made services, from places with no privacy to places that sometimes provide no company.

Foreword

But it would be naïve to think, against this more positive backdrop, that there is no need for the 'special' consideration and interventions described in this book. Just beneath the surface, the after-images of those negative stereotypes can still be seen, haunting efforts to integrate people and to protect their rights to information, to sexual rights and to respect. The rhetoric may have changed but the reality of living in fractured communities is no bed of roses. People with disabilities are still bullied and harassed or teased and infantilised so that doing nothing is not an option, it leaves people vulnerable to being pushed back into powerless and stigmatised sexual roles. That is why this book is so important, because it distils the lessons of this movement at a time of insecurity and change in the way public services are provided.

The book provides down to earth advice and examples that bridge this significant fracture line. People tend to position themselves at either end of a continuum, advocating protection or choice as if these were polar opposites and as if choosing one should deprive a person of the other. But most citizens expect to make choices about their sexual lives and to be protected from sexual abuse in equal measure. They want to be empowered so that they can both respect but also sometimes move on from the values of their parents or their culture.

Mostly we all want to be well informed and supported so that we can make safe choices and we want our social networks to be involved in setting helpful norms, recognising the points where, as friends or family they should be stepping up, or stepping back. There is no reason why people with learning disabilities should not be seen as part of 'most people' in this regard and this book provides the information that will equip those who advocate for them towards that goal.

There have been important shifts of emphasis along this journey, many of them dictated by men and women with learning disabilities themselves. Men and women's issues have been more clearly differentiated (McCarthy, 1999). Same sex relationships have been given proper recognition (Cambridge, 1997) as has the imperative for safer sexual practices (Cambridge & Brown, 1997). We have seen how important it is to establish a safe space for personal care (Carnaby & Cambridge, 2006) and to be sensitive to the more informal sexual culture created by service settings, and by the often one-sided relationships that people with learning disabilities develop with staff members (Thompson *et al*, 1997). Acknowledgment of sexual abuse has also been important because it informed and provided one impetus for the formalising of 'safeguarding' provision within adult social care services (Brown *et al*, 1995). Moreover it has

Foreword

also been important to develop expertise and commitment to working with men with learning disabilities who are at risk of committing sexual offences because this provides support to some high risk, but nonetheless very vulnerable men (Thompson & Brown, 2007).

Michelle McCarthy and David Thompson have been central to these developing lines of work. Michelle's work on women's sexuality and sexual health issues has done more than any other to paint their lives as they actually are, not as we might wish them to be. Her work is honest and inspiring. It does not idealise but challenges the lack of attention that is often paid to women with learning disabilities, to their real experiences of sex that is often rushed, forced or peremptory. This has led to far more support for women's choices in their relationships with men, with women, and in relation to their sexual health as in managing their periods, contraceptive options and menopause (McCarthy, 2002). Through this work Michelle has brought women with learning disabilities back into the mainstream in relation to their sexual health and safety from domestic violence and she grounds this in a strong feminist perspective.

David Thompson's work with men over the years (2001) including with men who are at risk of sexually offending, asks searching questions about male sexuality and its impact on women, and on other men. It opens up areas of discussion frankly and directly so that professionals come to see these men, whose behaviour might otherwise be stigmatised or dismissed in a more balanced way: this means that the risk their behaviour poses is neither minimised nor allowed to obscure their own vulnerability and humanity.

This book is a balanced and well grounded contribution to the development of good practice in this most challenging area. Many individuals and organisations (for example Respond, Ann Craft Trust, FPA, Sexuality Support Team (formerly Consent), Voice UK, The Tavistock Institute) have contributed to this developing area of work and this is a good place to thank them, alongside the authors of these chapters for their contribution over the past thirty years. These agencies and individuals have been visionary in refusing to go along with devaluing ways of working with people with learning disabilities, especially those whose sexuality gives rise to ethical challenges and dilemmas. They reject the old ways of squashing these issues or of fudging them because these often led to people being blamed or even incarcerated for expressing their sexuality in the only ways open to them. Instead they have chosen to address, research and inform people with learning disabilities, and the professionals and family members that support them.

Foreword

The chapter writers draw on many years of shared experience in this field and this book represents distilled wisdom as a result of their work and of their sensitivity to the many individuals with learning disabilities whose lives they have influenced. Perhaps the book also represents an opportunity to pass the baton from one generation to the next as these issues get taken forward into new service models and new times.

I recommend this book to you. I hope it will enable you to support people towards having sexual lives that are safe, respected and respectful. When there are difficult issues to be faced, I hope you will reach for it to help you address these with honesty and humanity.

Shakespeare *et al* (1992) coined a phrase which encapsulates what we should be aiming for on behalf of people with learning disabilities, it is that they should be helped to attain 'sexual citizenship', a concept echoed by Lesseliers *et al* in Chapter 6 when they say that people want to be 'agents in their own lives'. This book represents a very significant step towards reaching that goal.

Hilary Brown
Professor of Social Care
Canterbury Christ Church University
August 2010

Brown H (1994) An ordinary sexual life? A review of the normalisation principle as it applies to the sexual options of people with learning disabilities. *Disability and Society* 9 (2) 123–144.

Brown H, Stein J & Turk V (1995) The sexual abuse of adults with learning disabilities: Report of a second two year incidence survey. *Mental Handicap Research* 8 (1) 3–24.

Brown H & Turk V (1992) Defining sexual abuse as it affects adults with learning disabilities. *Mental Handicap* 20 (2) 44–55.

Cambridge P (1997) *HIV, Sex and Learning Disability: A staff training and sex education resource for working on HIV and with men with learning disabilities who have sex with men*. Brighton: Pavilion.

Cambridge P & Brown H (1997) *HIV and Learning Disability*. Kidderminster: British Institute of Learning Disabilities.

Carnaby S & Cambridge P (2006) *Intimate and Personal Care for People with Learning Disabilities*. London: Jessica Kingsley.

Craft A (1987) *Mental Handicap and Sexuality: Issues and perspectives*. Tunbridge Wells: Costello.

Craft A (1994) *Practice Issues in Sexuality and Learning Disabilities*. London: Routledge.

Craft M & Craft A (1978) *Sex and the Mentally Handicapped*. London: Routledge and Kegan Paul.

Fanstone C (2005) *Sex and the law as it affects people with learning disabilities: A practical guide*. London: FPA.

McCarthy M (1999) *Sexuality and women with learning disabilities*. London: Jessica Kingsley.

McCarthy M (2002) Going through the menopause: Perceptions and experiences of women with intellectual disabilities. *Journal of Intellectual and Developmental Disability* **27** (4) 281–295.

McCarthy M (2003) Drawing a line between consented and abusive sexual experiences: The complexities for women with learning disabilities. *Journal of Adult Protection* **5** (3) 34–40.

Thompson D (2001) Is Sex a Good Thing for Men with Learning Disabilities? *Tizard Learning Disabilities Review* **6** (1).

Thompson D & Brown H (2007) *Response-ability: working with men with learning disabilities who have abusive or unacceptable sexual behaviours*. Brighton: Pavilion Publishing.

Thompson D, Clare I & Brown H (1997) Not such an 'ordinary' relationship: The role of women support staff in relation to men with learning disabilities who have difficult sexual behaviour. *Disability and Society* **12** (4) 573–592.

Shakespeare T, Gillespie-Sells K & Davies D (1996) *The sexual politics of disability: Untold desires*. London: Cassell.

Contributors

Natasha Alexander PhD is a senior clinical psychologist at Newham Primary Care NHS Trust. Her clinical work and research interests include staff consultation, sexuality and sexual behaviour, self-injury and psychiatric rehabilitation.

Sandra Baum PhD is a consultant clinical psychologist at Newham Primary Care NHS Trust and she is also a qualified systemic psychotherapist. Her clinical work and research interests focus on using systemic approaches with families and staff teams and in improving services for parents with learning disabilities.

Paul Cambridge is a senior lecturer in learning disability, social work team, School of Social Policy, Sociology and Social Research, University of Kent at Medway. Paul has researched and written on the sexuality of men with learning disabilities. He has provided consultancy and training to staff, in addition to direct sex education with men with learning disabilities.

Claire Fanstone is the training manager for the FPA and trains professionals working with people with learning disabilities in sexual health issues. She is co-author of *Learning Disability and Sexuality*, and *Learning Disabilities, Sex and the Law* both published by the FPA.

Seema Fitzwater is a sexual health worker and trainee counsellor and has worked with adults with learning disabilities for the past 20 years both in London and New Delhi, India. At the Sexuality Support Team in Hertfordshire Partnership NHS Foundation Trust, she works directly with women and provides staff training. She has developed a service for parents with learning disabilities. She has a strong interest in cultural issues and has supported Asian clients with learning disabilities with arranged marriages.

Deborah Kitson worked as a social worker with adults and children with learning disabilities before focusing specifically on issues of abuse. She has been the director of the Ann Craft Trust since 2002.

Contributors

Joan Lesseliers PhD is a lecturer at University College Ghent, Department of Social Work and Welfare Studies, Association Ghent University. Joan is a sociologist with a PhD in the area of educational sciences. Her other research interests include institutionalisation and quality of life issues for people with learning disabilities.

Michelle McCarthy PhD is a senior lecturer in learning disability, Tizard Centre, University of Kent. Michelle has a long standing interest in working with women with learning disabilities on matters of sexuality and reproductive health. She teaches and researches in these areas and has written extensively on these topics.

Angela Mallett was a deputy head teacher at Shepherd School. This school had an international reputation for its work with young people with learning disabilities on sexual issues. In 2006 she produced *Bodyworks*, a sex education resource for those working with students with profound and multiple learning disabilities. She continues to support parent sex education groups at Oak Field School, Nottingham.

Jane Noonan is a sexual health worker and counsellor for the Sexuality Support Team in Hertfordshire Partnership NHS Foundation Trust. Jane has worked with adults with learning disabilities for over 25 years in residential care and as a counsellor specialising in women's sexual health, relationships and issues of abuse. Jane is directly involved in supporting service users, staff and parents with these issues.

David Stewart OBE is head teacher of Oak Field School and Sports College. He has been working in the field of sexuality and learning disability for the last 30 years. He worked on the original *Living Your Life* with Ann Craft and has overseen the revised editions. David has also produced with colleagues a series of resources for students and parents.

David Thompson PhD is senior practice development manager at Social Care Institute for Excellence (SCIE). David's current work is to promote good practice in decision-making for adults who may have difficulties in making decisions themselves. For over 10 years he worked directly with men with learning disabilities on sexual issues. Their experiences informed the research and writing he has undertaken in this area.

Tom Van Hoey PhD Ed is an educator at Vormingswerk voor en Met Mensen met een verstandelijke beperking (VMG VZW), a service for people with learning disabilities in Belgium. Tom has a Masters in Educational Sciences and works directly with people with learning disabilities, their families and staff. He has a strong interest in protecting the rights of people with learning disabilities.

Geert Van Hove PhD Ed is an associate professor in the Faculty of Psychology and Educational Sciences, Department of Special Education, Ghent University Belgium. Geert's areas of expertise include disability studies and inclusive education.

Introduction

Michelle McCarthy and David Thompson

Introduction

The aim of this book is to serve as a guide to those who may be inexperienced in supporting people with learning disabilities with sexual issues. Readers may be relatives seeking ideas about how to address a particular matter for a family member with learning disabilities, but are perhaps more likely to be staff working in services. It may also be useful to those studying on courses which cover learning disability issues.

This is an introductory text covering the most common questions and concerns relating to sexuality and learning disabilities. It guides readers to the kinds of support they might reasonably be expected to give people with learning disabilities themselves. It also suggests when it may be useful to refer onto others for more specialist support.

People often feel uncomfortable and out of their depth when it comes to helping people with learning disabilities with sexual issues. There is a desire to find and involve someone more qualified or experienced. This is understandable, but the reality is that specialists are few and far between, waiting lists may be long or costs can be prohibitive. However, sometimes people with learning disabilities can and should be guided by those who already support them and this book aims to give people confidence to do just that. (A list of useful organisations is found on p39).

Reading this book will give you the following:

▶ Information about the context of people with learning disabilities' sexual lives. This includes information on the relevant laws within the UK, information on reproductive health and on sex education.

▶ Knowledge of the range of sexual relationships and sexual activity which people with learning disabilities may be involved in. This includes same sex relationships as well as heterosexual ones, masturbation, sex which may lead to pregnancy and sexual abuse.

▶ Greater confidence to support individuals. Many staff and relatives may be reluctant to involve themselves in an area of life that is usually private. They may be concerned about taking decisions or helping the person with learning disabilities to take decisions about matters which may have serious consequences. This book should help people to understand that they rarely have to take responsibility for such matters by themselves. Often there are established processes, policies and professionals to help them.

▶ Sources of further help. Each chapter ends with suggestions for further reading and useful resources if readers want to find out more.

Contexts

There are a number of contexts which shape work with people with learning disabilities on sexual issues. These are relevant regardless of people's level of ability or communication skills and their potential need for support with sexual issues.

Changes in services

The chapter on sexual opportunities, interests and choices identifies how the sexual lives of people with learning are largely shaped by the way services are organised. This covers the potential for consented relationships, to be sexually abused and to sexually abuse others.

Across schools, adult day opportunities and residential services the overwhelming direction of travel has been away from large segregated settings to more individualised services. The personalisation of adult social care is moving this agenda further forward with people with learning disabilities generally spending less time with other people with learning disabilities, and being supported by staff who may have fewer opportunities to learn from the experience of their peers, and less direct management supervision.

This change is having a direct impact on many people with learning disabilities in ways that are rarely recognised. Most relevant to the focus of this book is that the best opportunities for people with learning disabilities to make and maintain friendships, or to meet a partner and develop a sexual relationship are when they are able and supported to spend regular time with other people with learning disabilities. There is a huge risk that without careful attention

to the area of relationships, personalised services will lead to more isolation and loneliness which is already a common experience for many people with learning disabilities.

It is perhaps therefore not surprising that there has been a recent trend towards dating and friendship clubs for people with learning disabilities driven by people with learning disabilities themselves. These can be understood as different forms of shared services.

Related to the development of smaller services is that staff may have few chances to discuss issues with colleagues and to benefit from a wider experience of work with people with learning disabilities. Progressing work on sexual issues requires learning from others who may have knowledge of appropriate resources or where specialist advice can be and should be obtained.

Personal beliefs and cultural values

Staff members are very often role models for people with learning disabilities. They are typically seen as powerful and successful, with access to the things that many people with learning disability desire, including marriage, children, work, money, cars, respect and confidence (though the truth may be very different). This projection of power should require staff to be very conscious of the level of influence they can have, and this includes in relation to their morals and values regarding sexual issues. For example, if a staff member says that they do not believe in sex outside marriage, their colleagues are likely to see this as a personal belief, whilst a person with learning disabilities might understand it as always being unacceptable.

Therefore staff should be very aware, if sharing personal information and views, of what effect it could have on people with learning disabilities. This could be both positive and negative. For example, a staff member saying that it is OK to masturbate or indeed that they themselves do it can very powerfully challenge any perception that a person with learning disabilities may hold that it is wrong. Unfortunately some staff exploit their power in an attempt to impose morals and values, which go against sexual rights that are protected in law, for example, homophobic staff telling people with learning disabilities that gay sex is wrong.

In recent years there has been a growing respect of the diversity in race, culture and religion of people with learning disabilities. Consequently, many services are trying to provide support which is sensitive to the specific needs

Introduction

of black and other minority ethnic clients. Clearly, sexuality support should be no different in aiming to meet the individual needs of people with learning disabilities in the context of their own culture. However, it is perhaps the most difficult area in which to do so. The difficulties arise in the variety of cultural beliefs about sexuality i.e. which relationships and sexual activities are valued and which ones are not.

When providing sex education to a person with learning disabilities where cultural issues arise, it is worthwhile recognising that people with learning disabilities are often influenced by a range of cultures, rather than being defined by just one. They will share the cultural background of their family, but may experience different cultures from other people with learning disabilities and the staff who work with them. Television is also likely to be another strong influence. From these different influences the person with learning disabilities' own set beliefs will have been shaped. These may be at variance with the culture into which they were born.

Care should be taken before making assumptions about what any particular culture's beliefs about sexuality are. Further, there is often some diversity within cultures about sexual beliefs, so it may be wrong to assume a person with learning disabilities or their family hold the most orthodox beliefs of a particular religion, for example. Ideally, advice should be sought from a number of representatives of the culture. It is useful to check whether there are any specific values with respect to the sexuality of people with learning disabilities.

To avoid potential conflict from services and family carers, it is useful to start by recognising the shared commitment to the person with learning disabilities' well-being. Since, in practice, sexuality support generally prioritises safety issues, there are good grounds to proceed in a way that will satisfy all concerned. Perceived or actual cultural influences should not be accepted as an excuse to deny people with learning disabilities the skills to protect themselves from sexual abuse. Similarly they should not stand in the way of taking action to remove a person with learning disabilities from what might be an abusive situation (see for example the section on forced marriages in Chapter 1).

Being supported to work with individuals

Managers have the responsibility to ensure that staff feel supported when they are asked to undertake work of a difficult or sensitive nature. Supporting people with learning disabilities with their sexual lives definitely comes into this category. Training in the area of sexuality is certainly helpful (see list of organisations which provide training on p39) but both staff and managers need to be realistic about what it can achieve. It is unrealistic to expect that after attending a short course that staff will feel or be fully competent. It is more likely that they would have acquired more knowledge and feel more confident.

In addition to skills and knowledge, staff should only work with people with learning disabilities on sexual issues when they have the support of other staff and their managers. Formal guidelines and policies can be very helpful (see McCarthy & Thompson, 2007 for a full discussion of these). It is not reasonable, or safe, for staff to work in isolation. When individuals work alone on sexual issues, with little or no oversight from their peers or managers, it puts both them and people with learning disabilities at risk. The risks range from bad practice, misguided ideas and imposing their own values on other people, right through to sexual and other forms of abuse.

Another reason for ensuring training and support is given to staff who undertake sexuality work is that it demonstrates a responsibility for the work held by the whole service. This is an important message to those staff and family members who are anxious about it.

Parents of people with learning disabilities are often assumed by staff to be opposed to sex education, and indeed some are. However, research and anecdotal evidence suggests that the majority of parents welcome it. Some parents, like others, may wrongly assume that sex education means just teaching people with learning disabilities how to have sex. There may be a need to explain the broad context of the support, encompassing aspects of safety, personal development, relationships, consent and health education. Parents can be great allies for sexuality work. There are lots of examples of parents being involved as representatives on planning and support groups concerning sexual issues. Such groups can similarly help family members to feel supported and confident to address their relatives' needs in this area.

Confidentiality

When supporting people with learning disabilities with sexual issues it is essential to be clear about the boundaries of confidentiality before staring work. As much as is possible, the limits of confidentiality should be explained to people with learning disabilities.

The availability of confidentiality may enhance work with people with learning

Introduction

disabilities because it may foster feelings of trust and respect. This may in turn improve the quality of the work if the person feels able to refer to sexual issues that have arisen in their life. Confidentiality can also give people a sense of control over the information they may disclose. This is particularly significant for people with learning disabilities who will have had very many experiences of not having control in their lives.

All services will have some constraints on what confidentiality can be offered to people with learning disabilities. For example, the organisation may have its own policy to which staff must adhere or members of professional bodies may be bound to follow their codes of conduct. One requirement is the directive contained in the Children's Act (1989) which insists that the potential abuse of a child should always be reported immediately to social services.

It is inappropriate for individual workers to make a commitment not to share any information with particular colleagues within their organisation. This is because it would undermine the potential of supervision and leave the worker vulnerable to taking personal responsibility for the consequences of sharing or not sharing information. This responsibility must be held by the employing organisation.

The most difficult dilemmas in confidentiality can arise when there are disclosures of potential sexual abuse, risks to sexual health or the potential of a pregnancy. The critical decision is whether this should be shared outside of the organisation. This could be with the police, social services or a health body who are in a position to take action.

Under the Data Protection Act (1998) personal information about adults can not be shared outside an organisation without the person's consent where they have the capacity to make this decision. There are exceptions where a crime may have been committed or life may be at risk. Otherwise sharing can take place if this is believed to be in the person's best interests.

After a disclosure, management support may be essential to decide on the two key questions. First, whether the person understands the implications of what they have said and so their wishes regarding sharing or not sharing must be respected. Second, where a person is thought not to adequately understand the potential implications of their disclosure whether this should be shared with another agency.

Advice here is to share information with an appropriate agency where a person with learning disabilities or other vulnerable person is a risk unless there is a strong justification to do otherwise. Serious case reviews where people with learning disabilities have been badly abused or killed have often been very critical of decisions taken by organisations not to pass on the information they held (e.g. Flynn, 2007).

Safeguarding adults and children

It is not possible to address sexual issues with people with learning disabilities without considering the risk of sexual abuse. Chapter 8 shows how recent awareness has been that people with learning disabilities can be sexually abused and this is evident from the title of the landmark book edited by Hilary Brown and Ann Craft called, *Thinking the Unthinkable* (1989).

Knowledge of the many different contexts in which people with learning disabilities are sexually abused has grown. This includes:

- counting the sexual abuse that is perpetrated by men with learning disabilities against other people with learning disabilities
- the common sexual abuse of women with learning disabilities in relationships
- the lack of mutuality when a man with learning disabilities has sex with a another man
- forced marriages.

Responses to the potential sexual abuse of (and by) people with learning disabilities are generally led by adult and child protection policies and procedures. For example, *No Secrets* (2000) and *In Safe Hands* (2000) set out for England and Wales respectively how agencies should work together in response to the potential abuse of a vulnerable adult.

The recent review of *No Secrets* (2009) has challenged the practice of much adult protection work. It found that agency responses to the potential abuse of vulnerable adults were often experienced very negatively by the adult themselves. So instead of being grateful for being removed from an abusive situation, adults often complained about the experience being disempowering as professionals were making choices that they believed they should be making.

Introduction

This does not mean that people with learning disabilities should be left unsupported in sexually abusive situations. Rather care must be taken to consider how the process, now referred to as 'safeguarding adults', can give people with learning disabilities the skills to gain greater control over this and other areas of their lives.

The chapters

This book does not claim to be the only, or definitive, work on sexuality and learning disability. However, it does cover most of the issues that people could reasonably be expected to cover when engaging in sex education or sexuality support work with the majority of people with learning disabilities.

Chapter 1 by Claire Fanstone and David Thompson sets out in detail the relevant laws which impinge on the sexual lives of people generally, and people with learning disabilities in particular. They give clear direction on ways both the spirit and the letter of the law need to guide the decisions that are made about people's sexual lives.

Chapter 2 by Paul Cambridge addresses the issue of masturbation. Helping people with this form of sexual expression is very important. For those with more severe disabilities and those without partners it may realistically be the only form of sexual activity they can engage in. It is a common activity for people with learning disabilities as it is for the rest of the population. However, the fact that it is common, does not mean it is without problems and Paul Cambridge offers guidance when supporting people.

Chapter 3 by Michelle McCarthy deals with menstruation and menopause. Often in the past, these normal life experiences were not properly addressed for women with learning disabilities, and instead they were ignored or problematised. We know that many girls and women with learning disabilities need and value support from other women when it comes to understanding and managing their periods and Michelle McCarthy sets out how to do this.

Chapter 4 by Angela Mallet and David Stewart addresses the important area of sexuality support for those who have profound and multiple disabilities. This is based on their work with children with learning disabilities in schools. There is a great risk that this group of people's needs are totally overlooked. Most sex education materials implicitly or explicitly ignore them and this chapter seeks to redress that imbalance.

Chapter 5 by David Thompson outlines some of the opportunities, interests and choices for people with learning disabilities when they seek relationships or other forms of sexual activity. It examines some of the constraints people face, these include the effect of the physical environment, as well as the attitudes and practices of key people in the lives of people with learning disabilities.

Chapter 6 by Joan Lesseliers, Geert Van Hove and Tom Van Hoey is based on a piece of Belgian research, where people with learning disabilities were asked to talk about their personal and sexual relationships. This provides an important insight into the ways people with learning disabilities, who may be on the receiving end of sex education think and feel. Listening to people with learning disabilities is a prerequisite for getting support right.

Chapter 7 by Sandra Baum and Natasha Alexander focuses on pregnancy and parenting. All too often this is viewed purely negatively for women with learning disabilities but in this chapter the authors aim to give more balance to the debate, by examining ways in which women can be positively supported if they do wish to have a child. They provide practical advice based on their own work with women with learning disabilities who either wanted to get or were pregnant.

Chapter 8 by Deborah Kitson looks at how knowledge of the sexual abuse of both adults and children with learning disabilities has evolved. She gives clear guidance on what people should do if they have concerns or indeed knowledge that sexual abuse has taken place. It is informed by Deborah's leadership of the Ann Craft Trust which provides support to people with learning disabilities, their families and paid staff on the issue of abuse. This national charity is named after the pioneer of sexuality work with people with learning disabilities in the UK.

Chapter 9 by David Thompson looks at the other side of the coin i.e. people with learning disabilities who sexually abuse others, or who have other forms of unacceptable sexual behaviour. He outlines which responses by individuals, services and society are helpful and which are not.

Chapter 10 by Seema Fitzwater and Jane Noonan concludes the book by setting out some of the important principles and practices involved in sex education. They cover formal approaches to sexuality support, as well as ways of utilising the more informal opportunities that arise in day-to-day life. It is based on the direct experience of the authors providing sex education to people with learning disabilities both individually and in groups over many years with the Sexuality Support Team in Hertfordshire.

The Sexuality Support Team has changed names several times since it began providing specialist sex education support to people with learning disabilities in 1989. It was originally called the AIDS Awareness/Sex Education Project and is where the editors of this book first started working together and directly with people with learning disabilities on sexual issues. They remain indebted to those people with learning disabilities they worked with at that time for sharing such intimate details of their sexual lives.

References

Brown H & Craft A (Eds) (1989) *Thinking the Unthinkable: Papers on sexual abuse and people with learning difficulties*. London: FPA Education Unit.

Department of Health and Home Office (2000) *No Secrets: Guidance on developing and implementing multi-agency policies and procedures to protect vulnerable adults from abuse*. London: HMSO.

Flynn M (2007) *The Murder of Steven Hoskin: A serious case review – executive summary*. Cornwall: Cornwall Adult Protection Committee.

McCarthy M & Thompson D (2007) *Sex and the 3Rs: Rights, Responsibilities and Risks*. Brighton: Pavilion.

Welsh Assembly Government (2000) *In Safe Hands: Implementing adult protection procedures in Wales* [online]. Available at: www.wales.gov.uk.

Chapter 1

People with learning disabilities, sex and the law

Claire Fanstone and David Thompson

Introduction

For many people, sex can be a difficult subject to talk about. When you add to this people with learning disabilities who may or may not have capacity to consent, and then add in the legislation, it can become confusing. This chapter explains the laws about sex in the UK. These are as follows:

▶ The Sexual Offences Act (2003) which covers England and Wales

▶ The Sexual Offences (Northern Ireland) Order (2008)

▶ The Sexual Offences (Scotland) Act (2009)

Also important are the laws about people who may lack capacity to make some decisions. In England and Wales this is the Mental Capacity Act (2005) and in Scotland the Adults with Incapacity (Scotland) Act (2000). At time of writing there is no similar law in Northern Ireland. Differences in law will be explained but for detailed information the acts from each country should be read.

Ideally people with learning disabilities should have the opportunity for a pleasurable, fulfilling sex life, free from discrimination and harm. Sometimes the law, with its role of protecting the person, seems to want to restrict this. Understanding the intricacies of the legal system should not prevent any of us working with, or caring for people with learning disabilities, from seeing them as holistic beings with sexual needs and desires. Knowledge of the legal boundaries can help carers support people with learning disabilities to develop safe, loving relationships whilst protecting them from abuse.

Chapter 1 – People with learning disabilities, sex and the law

This chapter is divided into the following sections.

▶ Consent to sex

▶ Offences against people with mental disorder

▶ Sex involving children under 16

▶ Capacity to marry or enter a civil partnership

Consent to sex

Key points
▶ The legal age of consent to sex is 16.

▶ Everyone who is 16 or over is assumed to have capacity to consent to sex, unless there is evidence to suggest otherwise.

▶ Some people with learning disabilities will need support to make their own decisions about sex.

▶ A small number of people with severe and profound learning disabilities will never be able to legally consent to sex.

This section looks at adults giving consent to sexual activities. Assessing whether someone has the capacity to consent or not can often be a difficult issue for anyone working with or caring for someone with a learning disability. It is legal for anyone aged 16 or over to engage in consensual sexual activity. This is true for all UK countries, including Northern Ireland, which most recently equalised their ages of consent for heterosexual and homosexual sex. It is perhaps worth noting that the average age of first heterosexual intercourse is 16 for men and women (Wellings, 2001).

The definition of consent within the Sexual Offences Acts covering England, Wales and Northern Ireland is as follows:

'A person consents if he agrees by choice and has the freedom and capacity to make that choice' (Sections 74 and 3 respectively).

Chapter 1 - People with learning disabilities, sex and the law

For Scotland, it is put more simply as 'free agreement' (Section 12).

Table 1.1 identifies the major sexual offences together with the maximum penalties that apply in the different parts of the UK. These apply regardless of whether the victim has learning disabilities. Other sexual offences include exposure, voyeurism, and causing a person to engage in a sexual activity with another person.

Table 1.1

Offence	Maximum prison sentence (UK countries)	Details
Rape	Life (all UK countries)	Rape is now the only sexual offence that can only be committed by a man, as it is defined as the intentional penetration with a penis of the vagina, anus or mouth of another person, without that person's consent. Rape is always committed when penetration occurs with a child under the age of 13.
Assault by penetration	Life (all UK countries)	This has the same definition as rape apart from the penetration of the vagina or rectum can be carried out by males or females with a part of the body or an object.
Sexual assault	10 years (England and Wales) Life (Scotland)	Sexual assault is any kind of intentional sexual touching of someone else without their consent. It includes touching (sexually) any part of their body, clothed or unclothed, either with any part of the body or with an object.

Everyone who is 16 and over should be assumed to have capacity to consent under the first principle of the Mental Capacity Act (2005) covering England and Wales. Some people with learning disabilities may be able to consent to sex if they receive support and education. The second principle of the Mental Capacity Act requires people to have all possible support to make their own decisions. Sex education plays an important role here. For example, Murphy found that 'people with learning disabilities who had had sex education were more knowledgeable and less vulnerable than others' (2003).

Therefore an educational approach to assessment of capacity is needed. Assessment of capacity to consent to sex can be undertaken by people close to the person with the learning disability who can understand their comprehension level and learning needs. For example, this could be a family carer or experienced support worker. At times it may be necessary to refer to professionals with knowledge in this area including psychologists. There are some useful tools to support this process listed at the end of this chapter.

Offences against people with mental disorder

Key points
- ▶ There are offences that recognise the vulnerability of people with learning disabilities to sexual abuse, and these apply to all people who have a mental disorder.
- ▶ It is illegal for care workers to engage in sexual activity with someone with a learning disability who they provide services to.

There is extra protection for people with learning disabilities regarding consent in each of the sexual offences acts under offences against people with 'mental disorder'. These laws recognise that while some people with learning disabilities may have an understanding of sex and its consequences, in some situations their ability to make a choice may be undermined by the power of the person seeking to have sex with them.

England, Wales and Northern Ireland
In England, Wales and Northern Ireland, people with learning disabilities (and other people with a 'mental disorder') may lack capacity to choose whether to agree to sexual activity because:

- ▶ they lack sufficient understanding of the nature, or reasonably foreseeable consequences of the sexual activity, or for any other reason, or
- ▶ they are unable to communicate their choice.

Guilt is dependent on the potential perpetrator knowing, or where it is reasonable to expect them to know, that the person has a mental disorder, and because of it is unlikely to be able to refuse. These are referred to as *offences against persons with mental disorder impeding choice*.

There has been some recent case law in this specific area (C v R [2009] UKHL 42 (30 July 2009)). The case involved a man who put his penis in the mouth of a woman who had schizo-affective disorder. The verdict was that she did not have the capacity at the time to refuse for reasons related to her mental disorder.

This is an important finding as it confirms that in some situations a person with learning disabilities may be able to make an informed decision about being involved in a specific sexual act with a specific person, but in others this may not be the case. Practically this could mean, for example, that a person with learning disabilities could have the ability to consent to sex with another person with learning disabilities but not with a powerful man without learning disabilities.

The vulnerability of people with learning disabilities to agree to sex because of what they are told will happen if they either agree or disagree is also recognised. This is referred to in law as *inducements, threats and deception*. Again to prove guilt the potential perpetrator needs to know, or could reasonably be expected to know that the person has a mental disorder.

Examples of inducements could include giving gifts or money, or promising presents or marriage to the victim. Deception could be telling lies such as 'all your friends do this' or 'you'll get ill if you don't'. Threats might include 'I'll tell your parents' or 'I'll hurt your friend'.

Scotland

The Scottish law in this area is different. It says that a person with mental disorder cannot consent to any sexual activity if 'by reason of mental disorder, the person is unable to do one or more of the following:

a. understand what the conduct is
b. form a decision as to whether to engage in the conduct or as to whether the conduct should take place
c. communicate any such decision' (Section 17).

There is no requirement that the potential perpetrator should be aware that the person has a mental disorder.

Sexual abuse by care workers

All countries make it illegal for people who work with people with learning disabilities to have sex with them. **Table 1.2** identifies the different offences and maximum sentences.

Table 1.2: Sexual offences involving care workers

England, Wales and Northern Ireland

Sexual activity with a person with a mental disorder (maximum sentence 10 years)

Causing or inciting sexual activity (maximum sentence 10 years)

Sexual activity in the presence of a person with a mental disorder (maximum sentence seven years)

Causing a person with a mental disorder to watch a sexual act (maximum sentence seven years)

Scotland

Sexual abuse of a mentally disordered person (maximum sentence five years)

The definition of 'care worker' is wide and includes:

▶ people in regular face-to-face contact with people with learning disabilities who are providing services in connection with their learning disabilities

▶ staff from NHS, social services, private and voluntary agencies.

This definition covers all types of care that the person with a learning disability may have. As well as more obvious staff such as day centre and residential workers, it can also include people like therapists, cleaners, taxi drivers, gardeners and caretakers.

These offences also apply to volunteers working with people with learning disabilities (except in Scotland). In all countries, it needs to be shown that the care worker knew, or it would be reasonable to expect them to know that the person had a mental disorder. Here the potential consent of the person with learning disabilities is not taken into consideration because of compliance, brought about by the position of trust held by a care worker, may be evident. This is not the same as free consent. So, regardless of consent, these offences apply.

The laws relating to people with mental disorder should not prevent care workers from providing legitimate sex and relationships education to people with learning disabilities. Education should be carried out in a way that is appropriate for each individual. For example, if it is thought necessary to directly teach a person with learning disabilities how to masturbate, workers should ensure that all sex education work is recorded and that legitimate reasons for using sensitive materials are discussed as part of an individual's care plan. This recording should be monitored and kept by the organisation employing the staff carrying out the work. This provides a defence against allegations of possible sexual abuse.

Sex involving children under 16

Key points

- Non-consensual sexual offences such as rape, assault by penetration and sexual assault apply to everyone, regardless of age.

- Sexual activities with young people aged 12 and under are deemed absolute offences as under-13 year olds cannot consent in law.

- The law recognises that in some situations children 13 years old and over can consent to sex, although this is still an offence for under-16 year olds. Prosecution is most likely if it involves an adult over 18 and 16 in Scotland.

Sexual offences, which require evidence that a person did not consent apply equally to young people under the age of 16. However, any sexual activity with children under 13 is deemed as an absolute offence, as in law they do not have capacity to consent. The defendant can not argue that the child consented, nor can they argue that they did not know that they were under 13. There is some acceptance in law that children who are 13 or over may, in some situations, be able to consent to sexual activity despite being under the legal age of consent, which is 16. In practice, the law usually turns a blind eye to sex involving two older children that is understood to be consented.

Scotland is unique in having a specific offence which covers consented sex between two older children (Section 37). Older children with learning disabilities may be less able than their non-disabled peers to make informed decisions about sex before they turn 16.

All countries have offences which are concerned with adults sexually exploiting older children (under the age of 16). In England, Wales and Northern Ireland this is if the adult is 18 or over, in Scotland it is 16 or over. They apply regardless of the consent of the older child. The defendant can argue that they had a reasonable belief that the child was 16 or over. This is different to sexual offences involving children under 13 where a similar defence is not allowed.

There are also offences in each country referred to as abuse of trust. They cover situations where adults are employed to provide a service to young people under the age of 18 and it includes teachers, youth workers and residential care workers. These offences are committed regardless of the consent of the young person. A defence of not knowing the young person was under 18 is allowed.

Family relationships

All countries have laws that forbid sexual relationships between family members regardless of the age and consent of the people involved. They make sex illegal with parents, grandparents, children, grandchildren, brothers, sisters, uncles, aunts, nephews and nieces. Scotland differs in only criminalising heterosexual family relationships in the Incest and Related Offences (Scotland) Act (1986). The genders of the people involved are not a feature of the comparative laws in other parts of the UK. For example, sex between a father and a 20-year-old son with learning disabilities would be covered by these laws. In Scotland, parental relationships are included under abuse of trust laws. Here it is an offence for anyone with parental responsibility to have sex with their child if they are under the age of 18.

Capacity to marry or enter a civil partnership

Key points

▶ The contract of marriage is not difficult. Many people with learning disabilities have the capacity to get married.

▶ There are laws to protect people with learning disabilities being forced to marry.

▶ Entering a civil partnership is an option available to people with learning disabilities.

▶ Decisions about marriage or civil partnership cannot be made by other people in the best interests of people with learning disabilities.

The chapter on sexual interests, opportunities and choices (see page 81) shows that an increasing number of people with learning disabilities are getting married. Too often people with learning disabilities in relationships have been told that they are unable to get married. Alternatively, this might not have been explicitly stated, but practical support to allow this to happen is denied. This law covering what is required to consent to marriage goes back a long way. A recent case looked at the key judgements in this area (Sheffield City Council v E [2004] EWHC 2808 Fam (2 December 2004)). This gave the following guidance.

▶ 'It is not enough that someone appreciates that he or she is taking part in a marriage ceremony or understand its words.

▶ He or she must understand the nature of the marriage contract.

▶ This means that he or she must be mentally capable of understanding the duties and responsibilities that normally attach to marriage.

▶ That said, the contract of marriage is in essence a simple one, which does not require a high degree of intelligence to comprehend.

▶ There are thus, in essence, two aspects to the inquiry whether someone has capacity to marry. (1) Does he or she understand the nature of the marriage contract? (2) Does he or she understand the duties and responsibilities that normally attach to marriage?

▶ The duties and responsibilities that normally attach to marriage can be summarised as follows: marriage, whether civil or religious, is a contract formally entered into. It confers on the parties the status of husband and wife, the essence of the contract being an agreement between a man and a woman to live together and to love one another as husband and wife, to the exclusion of all others. It creates a relationship of mutual and reciprocal obligations, typically involving the sharing of a common home and a common domestic life and the right to enjoy each other's society, comfort and assistance' (Section 141).

The case summary also says that the person's choice of partner is irrelevant in making decisions about their capacity to marry, for example, whether others think it is a good or bad pairing.

In practice it is the person conducting the marriage ceremony that needs to make a decision about a person's capacity to marry. Their decision can be challenged in the courts.

Forced marriage

There has been some recent attention given to forced marriages involving people with learning disabilities (see Chapter 8). The Forced Marriages (Civil Protection) Act (2007) says that a person is forced into a marriage if another person forces them to enter into a marriage without their free and full consent. This includes situations when people marry because they are afraid of what might happen to either themselves or other people. It covers marriages which have taken place anywhere in the world and this act gives powers to prevent marriages and to take action on behalf of people who are in a forced marriage.

Civil partnerships

Since 2005 it has been possible for two women or two men to enter a civil partnership across the UK. At time of writing it is not known if any people with learning disabilities have chosen to make this commitment. The Civil Partnership Act (2004) says that civil partnership between two people may be void, if:

▶ 'either of them did not validly consent to its formation (whether as a result of duress, mistake, unsoundness of mind or otherwise)

- at the time of its formation, either of them, though capable of giving a valid consent, was suffering (whether continuously or intermittently) from mental disorder of such a kind or to such an extent as to be unfitted for civil partnership' (Section 50).

Limits on 'best interests' decisions

Where a person with learning disabilities lacks capacity to make a particular decision, the Mental Capacity Act (2005) covering England and Wales, sets out how decisions should be made in their best interests. However, it says that there are some decisions which cannot be made on someone's behalf. These include:

- consenting to a marriage or civil partnership
- consenting to have sexual relationships
- consenting to a decree of divorce on the basis of two years separation
- consenting to the dissolution of a civil partnership.

Conclusion

The updated sexual offences laws have tried to balance the potential of some people with learning disabilities to consent to sex with their vulnerability to sexual abuse. This is a difficult balance for carers to achieve in their role of supporting people with learning disabilities with relationships. Where there are questions about the consent of a person with learning disabilities, care should be taken not to over-use the law as a reason to prevent sexual opportunities, for example, to stop contact because it might be against the law. This is different to situations where there is no doubt that the person lacks capacity to consent or it involves sex with a care worker.

Where there are concerns about a person with learning disabilities' ability to consent to sex with someone where a lawful sexual relationship is possible, this should be appropriately assessed and, if necessary, support provided to enhance their ability make their own decisions.

References

C v R [2009] UKHL 42 (30th July 2009)

Murphy G (2003) Capacity to consent to sexual relationships in adults with learning disabilities. *Journal of Family Planning and Reproductive Healthcare* **29** (3) 148–149.

Seffield City Council v E [2004] EWHC 2808 Fam (2 December 2004)

Wellings K (2001) Sexual behaviour in Britain: early heterosexual experience. *The Lancet* **358** 1843–1850.

Further reading

British Medical Association and The Law Society (2004) *Assessment of Mental Capacity: Guidance for doctors and lawyers*. London: BMJ Books.

Department of Health (2001) *Consent: A guide for people with learning disabilities*. London: Department of Health.

Dodd K, Turk V & Christmas M (2007) *Exploring Sexual and Social Understanding: An illustrated pack designed for working with people with learning disabilities*. Birmingham: BILD.

Fanstone C & Andrews S (2009) *Learning Disabilities, Sex and the Law: A practical guide (Second edition)*. London: FPA.

Fraser J (2010) *Sexual Knowledge and Behaviour: An assessment tool for use with young people with learning disabilities*. Cumbria: Me and Us.

Harbour A (2008) *Children with Mental Disorder and the Law: A guide to law and practice*. London: Jessica Kingsley Publishers.

Her Majesty's Stationery Office (2003) *Explanatory Notes to the Sexual Offences Act (2003)*. London: Crown Copyright.

Sexual Offences Act 2003 [online]. Available on: http://www.opsi.gov.uk/si/si2010/uksi_20100207_en_1.

Sexual Offences (Scotland) Act 2009 [online]. Available on: http://www.opsi.gov.uk/legislation/scotland/acts2009/asp_20090009_en_1.

Sexual Offences (Northern Ireland) Order 2008 [online]. Available on: http://www.opsi.gov.uk/si/si2008/draft/ukdsi_9780110800936_en_1.

Relevant contacts

Ann Craft Trust is a UK-based organisation working with staff in the statutory, independent and voluntary sectors to protect people with learning disabilities who may be at risk from abuse. They also provide advice and information to parents and carers who may have concerns about someone that they are supporting.
Tel: 0115 9515400
Website: www.anncrafttrust.org

FPA is a sexual health charity, which offer training for professionals working with people with learning disabilities.
Tel: 0207 608 5276
Website: www.fpa.org.uk

Respond provides a range of services to both victims and perpetrators of sexual abuse who have learning disabilities. Support for families, carers and professionals is also provided.
Tel: 0207 383 0700
Website: www.respond.org.uk

Sexuality Support Team (formerly Consent) offers a range of services to people with learning disabilities, including enabling informed choices, sexual health, issues of HIV risks and working with people with learning disabilities who have been sexually abused or perpetrated sexual abuse.
Tel: 01923 670796
Website: www.hertspartsft.nhs.uk

Voice UK provides telephone support for adults and children with learning disabilities who have been abused and for their families and carers.
Tel: 0845 122 8695
Website: www.voiceuk.org.uk

Chapter 2

Masturbation

Paul Cambridge

Chapter 2 – Masturbation

Introduction

Masturbation is a key consideration when supporting the sexuality of people with learning disabilities for the following key reasons:

▶ it is the most frequent form of sexual expression including for people with learning disabilities

▶ many of the difficulties reported in relation to sexuality and people with learning disabilities concern masturbation

▶ responding to masturbation can create tensions between the rights of service users and the responsibilities of carers

▶ sexual self-stimulation is likely to be the only form of sexual expression available to people with profound and multiple learning disabilities.

Despite this, little guidance exists for carers on how to respond effectively when masturbation presents as a support challenge. The aim of this chapter is therefore to provide pointers for responding to some of the most frequently experienced situations concerning masturbation.

Background

Sometimes people with learning disabilities experience difficulty expressing their sexuality through masturbation and a number of factors help explain this. Many people with learning disabilities have been told or believe that masturbation is wrong and consequently feel ashamed of or deny such behaviour. People with learning disabilities are also unlikely to have received good education and advice about masturbation, including how and where to do it and that it is an OK thing to do. The ways shared and private spaces are organised in services can also create difficulties. Moreover, problems associated with masturbation are generally more visible when they concern men than women, with the needs of women with learning disabilities remaining relatively neglected in relation to masturbation (McCarthy, 1999).

Staff and carers tend to identify a range of concerns in relation to masturbation (see Cambridge *et al*, 2003 for a more detailed discussion).

- The person does not know how to masturbate appropriately, for example, they stimulate themselves sexually by rubbing their vagina or penis through their clothes or against objects.
- The person is thought to be unable to masturbate effectively, for example, a man might have difficulties with having an erection or ejaculation or a woman might not be able to reach an orgasm – possibly causing frustration.
- The person is masturbating too much, for example, they are doing it too frequently or for too long and as a consequence miss out on other opportunities or activities, or cause soreness.
- The person is masturbating when other people are around, for example, doing it in a public place or a shared room in a service.
- The person is using inappropriate objects to aid masturbation, there may be a risk or evidence of injury.

The factors which influence how staff and carers interpret and respond to masturbation are therefore complex.

Not recognising that masturbation can be important for people with learning disabilities

In the past it was considered that people with learning disabilities did not need to know how to masturbate or staff and carers were too embarrassed to provide advice about masturbation. The only message that people often received was that masturbation was wrong. Staff and carers also need support and guidance about how to respond positively and sexuality policies or individual care guidelines are helpful in this regard. Attending sexuality training can also help staff feel more confident to provide support.

Lack of effective and accessible sex and relationships education

Special line drawings and videos have been produced which show masturbation for education with people with learning disabilities. However, staff and carers may not know how to get hold of these or feel able to use them confidently and effectively. People with more profound and multiple learning disabilities are even less likely to have received relevant sex education partly because there are few such materials available.

Lack of privacy

The ways services and support for people with learning disabilities are organised heavily influence what happens in people's lives. For example, in congregate service provisions such as day centres and residential services, many spaces are shared. This limits privacy and can make it difficult for someone to find an appropriate place to masturbate. The lives of people with learning disabilities are also often highly scrutinised, with the result that their masturbation is likely to be more known about than other people.

Individual needs

Problems associated with masturbation might be attributed to attempts to communicate, to avoid particular people or situations or to gain attention. Whilst such factors may be significant, they also risk distracting attention from a person's need to express their sexuality safely and appropriately.

Gender and culture

Masturbation is generally reported to be more of an issue for men than for women with learning disabilities. This is because the sexuality of women with learning disabilities is generally less visible and more hidden, including masturbation. For women with learning disabilities there may be additional embarrassment and reluctance to talk about the subject. There are also culturally specific views about masturbation which may need to be taken account of when supporting someone from a minority ethic or cultural group.

Information

When masturbation presents as a problem, it is important to find out as much as possible about what is happening.

How is the person masturbating?
Questions for a woman with learning disabilities may include 'does she directly stimulate her clitoris, vagina or breasts' and 'is this done above or beneath clothing'? For a man: 'does he get an erection, get his penis out, use his hand or ever ejaculate'? If masturbation is happening in a private place such as a bedroom or toilet, such questions are likely to be more difficult to answer, but indirect evidence such as the presence of semen on sheets may prove helpful. If possible, the best approach will be to elicit accounts directly from the person through individual sex education.

Is there a pattern to the masturbation?
It is helpful to clarify the actual behaviour and its context and check if anyone else has any ideas about what is happening and what might explain the behaviour. This will include considerations such as whether a particular response seems to be more effective than another and whether the behaviour varies between different places or times of the day or occurs if certain staff or service users are present.

Is this an indicator of sexual abuse?
Due to the high level of sexual abuse experienced by people with learning disabilities (McCarthy & Thompson, 1997; Murphy, 2007; Cambridge *et al*, 2010) it will also be important to consider the possibility that inappropriate masturbation is a sign that the person has or is being sexually abused, or is a way to communicate abuse.

Are there any other explanations?
Possible medical reasons may need to be checked out with a GP, including a vaginal, penile or urinary tract infection or a skin condition such as thrush or eczema. Sometimes medication can make it difficult for a man to masturbate effectively and some conditions such as Prader-Willi syndrome are associated with the immature development of the sexual organs, which may also make it difficult to masturbate.

Responding

The following case studies are taken from real situations, illustrating some of the challenges masturbation can present and suggesting possible responses.

Masturbation and self-injury

Case study

Anila is a young woman with severe learning disabilities who uses very little spoken language. The support staff use a small number of signs and some pictures to support communication. Her key worker has been worried for some time about blood found on Anila's sheets when changing her bed. Yesterday she found a coat hanger in the bed with dried blood on it. She was unable to find out from Anila where the blood had come from and removed the coat hanger before speaking with her manager.

Sometimes people with learning disabilities use inappropriate objects for sexual stimulation which risk injury. These may be inserted into the vagina or anus because the person has found that this is sexually stimulating or helps them achieve orgasm or ejaculation during masturbation.

In Anila's situation, her support worker took the correct action in removing an object which might be causing her injury. This idea could be checked out through individual work with Anila by monitoring or observation that respected her privacy (for example checking the sheets regularly when she is out of her room) and by speaking with others who provide support for her. Meanwhile, it would be sensible to provide Anila with the opportunity to use a safer object such as a soft dildo by leaving it on her bed. The possibility of past or current sexual abuse would also need to be considered (p46).

Masturbation during intimate care

Case study

Peter is a man with profound and multiple learning disabilities (PMLD) in his mid-30s living in a residential care home and he relies on staff for all aspects of his personal care. Three days a week are spent at a special care unit which is part of a local day centre. At the home team meeting a female support worker reports that Peter has recently been getting an erection and attempts to touch his penis when his continence pad is removed. This often happens when his penis and anus are washed using warm soapy water (using disposable wipes and protective gloves). No other home staff report that this has happened but when the manager checks at the day centre she finds that this had also happened with a male care worker there.

Much regular support work for people with PMLD revolves around routine tasks such as washing, bathing and continence care. People with PMLD are unlikely to know about masturbation and may be physically unable to masturbate. It is not uncommon for sexual arousal to take place when their continence pad is changed and the sexual parts of their bodies are washed. This may also be the only time that the sexual parts of their body are exposed and they have the opportunity to touch themselves sexually.

In Peter's situation, the support worker did the right thing in reporting her observations to the team. Finding out that it happened with the male worker at the day centre suggests it is less about one staff member than how intimate care is given. An idea would be for Peter to have time on his own after intimate care prior to a clean pad being secured, giving him the chance to explore himself sexually and touch his penis. His care plan should set this out and could for example, include what to do if he tries to touch himself when a member of staff is present. It could also set out verbal cues to be used such as 'you can touch now, Peter' (matched to his level of verbal understanding). The guidelines should also be clear about where Peter could be left alone safely and for how long.

Inability to masturbate effectively and inappropriate masturbation

Case study

Julie is a woman with Down's syndrome and moderate learning disabilities who exhibits some challenging behaviours including screaming and occasionally hitting staff. Once or twice a week Julie also displays sexually inappropriate behaviour, usually in the form of rubbing herself against a chair arm in the sitting room or less frequently against the bodies of male staff. When this happens, she is asked to leave the room or pushed away, with a reinforcing verbal cue that this is not allowed.

It is always important to consider the reasons for any challenging behaviour and records such as ABC charts should be kept to see if there are patterns to this, such as to avoid a particular situation, activity or person. It may also be to gain attention or to communicate that something is wrong, such as sexual abuse. Alternatively it might simply be the case that Julie has never received good sex education tailored to her needs and abilities and simply does this when she feels sexy or finds someone sexually attractive.

In Julie's situation the staff did the right thing in treating her sexual behaviour as unacceptable. However, it is also important to help her understand where and when such sexual behaviour is acceptable and this might involve guiding or asking her to go to her own room. Julie would also benefit from individual sex education focusing on appropriate and effective masturbation. Sex educational materials such as line drawings, videos or a model vagina and clitoris might prove helpful.

Masturbation and sexual fetish

Case study

Steve is a young man with autistic spectrum disorder. He collects pictures of babies in nappies and uses nappies and other baby things as part of masturbation. These have always been taken away from him by carers when they have been found in his room. When this happens he gets upset and withdraws and his behaviour can become more challenging.

Chapter 2 – Masturbation

This example is a reminder of how often carers know more about the private lives of people with learning disabilities than other people – people who are more able to hide their sexual interests. Other examples of sexual fetishes associated with masturbation include cross dressing and foot or shoe fetishes.

A starting point is to identify what the problem is – is it Steve's behaviour or the carers' knowledge or attitude towards it? Many men and women without learning disabilities enjoy sexual fetishes which cause no harm to anyone else and attempting to stop someone having a sexual fetish generally doesn't work. Moreover, it is likely to also be a violation of their rights to private and safe sexual expression. Sex education should instead pay attention to boundaries, responsibilities and consequences. For Steve this could mean finding ways to access nappies which don't involve stealing, having safe and secure storage in his bedroom where his baby things are kept when he is not using them so that carers and other users do not need to see them, how and when he can safely use nappies, how any negative effect of his sexual fetish on other people can be minimised, and what might happen if he discloses this to others. Often when people are given the space to express their sexual fetish appropriately, then its significance in their lives diminishes.

Pornography and masturbation

Many men and some women enjoy pornography whilst masturbating and if used in private by people with learning disabilities it should generally be seen as acceptable. Men with learning disabilities may need to be encouraged to keep it hidden in their rooms and not to show it to other people and may also need to understand that pornography rarely reflects what sex with another person is really like.

The chapter on sexual interests, opportunities and choices (see p81) advises against carers supporting men to obtain pornography, including where it is suggested as a possible solution for a man with learning disabilities who is experiencing problems masturbating. Suggesting the use of pornography is fraught with difficulties including whether someone would be interested in it, what kind of images they might like, whether they might be offended and whether it is likely to address existing problems effectively or cause new problems. The police should be involved if a man with learning disabilities is accessing or is in possession of illegal images of adults or children, for example sexual violence or paedophilia.

Conclusion

Services for people with learning disabilities should ideally have a sexuality policy to advise staff of their responsibilities and what to do in particular circumstances, including:

▶ what work they can do and when they need to get specialist advice

▶ what to do when they are exposed to a person with learning disabilities masturbating such as during intimate care or in a shared space

▶ how masturbation might be related to sexual abuse – either as a potential indicator of abuse or as a form of abuse when being done in front of people (including other people with learning disabilities and staff)

▶ the limits to individual work, such as not directly showing or helping someone to masturbate.

Whether or not a policy is available, staff should seek the advice of their line manager or supervisor with responses agreed and recorded in individual plans. This also allows information to be shared within and between teams and is necessary for consistent and considered responses.

The degree of a person's learning disability and their communication needs will affect how support and sex education linked to masturbation can be given. The help of specialists such as sex educators, psychologists or communication therapists will sometimes be needed.

Occasionally staff or family members may oppose advice and education about masturbation in the belief that it will lead to inappropriate sexual behaviour such as exposure. However, there is no evidence to suggest that ignoring difficult situations is more effective than providing information, direction and support.

This all underlines the importance of developing a collective vision and team approach which aims to empower people with learning disabilities to take control and make choices in their lives. Something as common and potentially harmless as masturbation has to be a focus of such work. It is also important to keep things in perspective and to remember that many people with learning disabilities enjoy masturbation as an ordinary part of their sexual lives without any problems. More importantly, everyone should have a right to masturbate as part of their sexual expression.

References

Cambridge P, Carnaby S & McCarthy M (2003) Responding to masturbation in supporting sexuality and challenging behaviour in services for people with learning disabilities. *Journal of Learning Disabilities* **7** (3) 251–266.

Cambridge P, Beadle-Brown J, Milne A, Mansell J & Whelton B (2010) Patterns of risk in adult protection referrals for sexual abuse and people with intellectual disability. *Journal of Applied Research in Intellectual Disabilities*. Published online.

McCarthy M (1999) *Sexuality and Women with Learning Disabilities*. London: Jessica Kingsley.

McCarthy M & Thompson D (1997) A prevalence study of sexual abuse of adults with intellectual disabilities referred for sex education. *Journal of Applied Research in Intellectual Disabilities* **10** (2) 105–124.

Murphy G (2007) Intellectual disabilities, sexual abuse and sexual offending. In: A Carr, G O'Reilly, P Noonan Walsh & J McEvoy (Eds) *The Handbook of Intellectual Disability and Clinical Psychology Practice*. London: Routledge.

Chapter 3

Menstruation and menopause

Michelle McCarthy

Introduction

Starting periods at puberty, having them regularly throughout life, then going through the menopause in middle age are normal and natural experiences for almost all women. This includes women with learning disabilities. Women with learning disabilities can best be supported by:

- being given clear information about what is happening to their bodies, at a level they can understand
- where necessary, being assisted with personal hygiene, in a respectful and positive manner
- being helped to understand that periods are normal, natural, and nothing to be frightened or ashamed of.

For the small group of women whose learning disabilities are in the severe and profound range and who cannot understand what is happening to them, they can best be supported by carers making them as comfortable as possible if they experience any physical pain or emotional changes.

For most women with learning disabilities their experience of starting, having and finishing their periods is broadly the same as for other women. The only exception to this is that women with learning disabilities generally tend to have a somewhat earlier menopause than most other women, and that women with Down's syndrome have a significantly earlier menopause (i.e. average age 46 years compared to 51 years in the general population). An earlier

menopause in women with Down's syndrome may be due to the fact that the ageing process generally appears to take place prematurely for people with this condition. Why women with learning disabilities, but without Down's syndrome have an earlier menopause is more difficult to determine, but may be due to the fact that women who have never given birth tend to have an earlier menopause than those who have.

Throughout history and across all cultures, women have generally preferred to talk to other women about their periods. There are obviously exceptions to this and some women have a male partner or male doctor who they may prefer to talk to. But generally speaking, all services should ensure that women with learning disabilities are supported by women staff when dealing with their periods. This replicates the situation in most families where it will be the mother or other female relative who support women with learning disabilities with their menstrual care.

Menstruation

When girls first start their periods (average age is around 11–12) it can be upsetting if they are not prepared in advance. It is always a good idea to talk to girls about what is going to happen to them as they go through puberty. A number of changes take place to a girl's body at this time, first changes to her body shape (and developing breasts is the most obvious change), then growing hair on her body. These kinds of changes tend to happen slowly and gradually, whereas the first period (which usually happens after the above changes) is an 'event'. Some cultures have celebrations to mark this occasion, but even where this is not so, it is always possible for mothers or other carers to be positive about it, to try to make the girl feel good about herself and proud that she is growing up.

Girls need to know that it can take a year or so for their periods to settle into a regular pattern (although some will be regular from the start). They also need to know that they will have a period roughly once a month until they reach middle age, when they will stop.

Menopause

This is often called the 'change of life' or just 'the change'. It happens in middle age (average age is 51), but unlike the onset of periods, it is not an 'event' but a long process. Hormone levels drop and this not only causes periods to cease, but hot flushes and emotional symptoms, such as mood swings, irritability, etc. Some women do not experience any problems with their menopause, but most will experience some symptoms which do cause them discomfort or distress. On average women will be aware of menopausal changes happening to their bodies for about four years.

Whilst some women experience an abrupt end to their periods, for most it tends to be that they become irregular, stop for while, then start again, and this pattern continues for some time. The pattern of blood flow may also change and become lighter or heavier than before. Over time, less bleeding, less often is generally what happens until periods stop altogether.

Supporting women with learning disabilities with their periods

There are three main areas of work:

- practical help
- education
- emotional/psychological support.

Practical help

This involves helping women to 'manage' their periods. This could include:

- trying out different kinds of sanitary protection to see which suits them best
- helping them buy the things they need and to have them ready for when they need them
- helping them change and dispose of the used pads appropriately

- helping them to manage any pain they may experience before or during their periods. This may be anything from simple painkillers and hot water bottles, to trying out alternative remedies (such as oil of evening primrose). Where pain or heavy bleeding is experienced over the long term, it will be necessary to support the woman in getting medical help. Often GPs will prescribe the contraceptive Pill for period problems and this may be a good option for some women. Only in rare cases will a hysterectomy be appropriate. Usually more minor surgical options such as removal of polyps or fibroids or endometrial ablation (where the lining of the womb is destroyed or removed) should be considered first.

- helping them to behave appropriately when they have a period, for example, not showing their sanitary pads or talking about their periods to everyone they meet. This doesn't mean they should be made to feel embarrassed or ashamed of having a period, but seeks to ensure that as far as possible, they behave as most other women do.

Education

This involves helping women understand what periods are and why they happen. This could include:

- explaining that only women and not men have periods and only for a certain time in their lives

- explaining what periods are for i.e. how they fit into a woman's reproductive system. However, such complex information can be difficult to simplify e.g. if someone is told women have periods 'so that one day they can have babies', this could cause confusion, fear or an unrealistic expectation of having a baby. It is not necessary for everyone to understand the details of why periods occur – young girls when they first start having periods usually do not know in great detail why, just that it is normal and healthy.

- explaining what other changes happen to the body when periods are coming for example not just bleeding, but perhaps putting on weight, sore or heavy breasts, spots, emotional and mood changes or abdominal and back pain.

Emotional/psychological support

This could include:

▶ finding out how women with learning disabilities feel about having periods

▶ finding out who they would like to support them and what kinds of support they would like

▶ trying to engender a positive view of periods. Many women, particularly older women, are raised to consider having periods as a dirty or shameful thing – carers could counterbalance this by giving more positive messages. It may be unrealistic to expect all women to have a positive view of periods, especially if they experience significant pain or discomfort. But where periods are not painful, it is not necessary to always think of them as a burden or unwelcome

▶ women carers sharing their own experience of having periods. It is helpful for women with learning disabilities who may have few other people to talk to about their periods to hear what carers think and feel about this shared experience. Remember that many women with learning disabilities will not be able to read magazines and access other kinds of written information.

Case study
Beth is a 14-year-old girl with learning disabilities. Her mother died a long time ago and she lives with her father and older brother. She has told her dad that she needs to see the doctor because she is not well but has been vague about the symptoms. She has not been putting some of her clothes in the family laundry basket but hiding them instead. Her teacher has noticed that Beth seems worried and irritable.

Who could help Beth and what should they do first? Consider what support she might need in the short and long term.

Supporting women with learning disabilities through the menopause

Having a learning disability does not necessarily mean women will have a different menopausal experience from other women. But there are some possible differences to consider. These differences tend to be emotional/psychological, cognitive, or social and suggest the areas where women may need support.

Emotional/psychological effects

Women with learning disabilities are as likely to experience mood swings, irritability and depression as other women. They may feel more anxious than other women due to their likely lack of knowledge and understanding about what is happening to them. They may live in group homes or other settings where they have relatively little privacy, which may be an additional stress. It is important that staff and family carers recognise the menopause as a possible cause of tension and difficulties for middle-aged women with learning disabilities and not jump to conclusions about 'challenging behaviour'.

Psychologically adjusting to the loss of their fertility and status as mothers is likely to be a different process for many women with learning disabilities compared to many other women. Certainly the emotional and psychological changes which are frequently raised in relation to other middle-aged women (e.g. the so-called 'empty nest' syndrome, which refers a loss of function, role and sense of usefulness) are rarely reported either by the women with learning disabilities or those close to them. Few women with learning disabilities get the chance to 'use' their fertility in the first place, therefore the loss of it is likely to impact on them differently, and for some, not at all. Added to this is the fact that many women with learning disabilities do not understand that the menopause does actually mean the end of a woman's fertility. However, there may be some women with learning disabilities who have always wanted to have children and who may need considerable support in coming to terms with the fact that this will now never happen.

Cognitive effects

Certain cognitive effects such as forgetfulness and an inability to concentrate are known to occur in some women in the menopausal years. If this happens to middle-aged women with learning disabilities, then it is important to recognise that these may be due to the menopause and not necessarily be related to the learning disability itself or to a general decline in intellectual ability. For women with Down's syndrome, where the early onset of dementia is considerably more common than it is for the general population, it may initially be difficult to determine what is causing the cognitive changes.

Social effects

As they grow older and go through the menopause, women with learning disabilities may be less affected by negative feelings related to their perceived loss of attractiveness and status in society than some other women. This is due to the fact that as disabled women they may have lived their whole lives being considered asexual and unattractive. This does not mean that those women with learning disabilities who are aware of these societal attitudes will not be upset at being considered unattractive. But it does mean that it is unlikely to become a particular issue in midlife. Other women with learning disabilities, particularly those with more severe learning disabilities, may well be unaware of societal attitudes. Many individual women with learning disabilities strive to make the most of their appearance, investing time, effort and money to present themselves in the best light they can and there is no reason why they should not be supported to do so into middle and old age.

Many women with learning disabilities will rely on other people for their information, support and access to health care. Their views on menstruation and the menopause are likely to be strongly influenced by those close to them. However few women with learning disabilities have any opportunities to discuss how they feel about their reproductive health and learn about other women's experiences. Supportive women carers and women's groups can play an important role in providing those opportunities.

Chapter 3 – Menstruation and menopause

> **Case study**
>
> Alice is a 43-year-old woman with Down's syndrome. She lives in a group home and visits her elderly parents most weekends. She has become very withdrawn and tearful and does not want to visit her parents anymore. Her key worker notices that Alice has several packets of sanitary pads piling up in her bedroom. When she asks Alice about this, Alice is very upset. She says she thinks she must be pregnant but is very confused about this as she hasn't had sex. She is afraid of what her parents will say when they find out.

Who could help Alice and what should they do first? Consider what support she might need in the short and long term.

Men with learning disabilities

Boys and men with learning disabilities should have some basic information about what periods are, why they happen and why they stop etc. As men obviously do not have personal experience of it, it may be more difficult to explain it to them than to women of the same ability level. If men with learning disabilities have close friendships with women and particularly if they have sexual relationships with women, they need to know how they can support women if or when the women are feeling uncomfortable or unhappy. This could be anything from fetching a hot water bottle or painkillers if she has period pains to respecting her wishes about having sex during a period.

Conclusion

In the past decade, research has been carried out to explore how girls and women with learning disabilities feel about their periods and the menopause. Regarding periods, Rodgers (2001a, 2001b) found that women with learning disabilities generally had a pervasive feeling of negativity. More recently Mason & Cunningham (2007) found similar findings with women with Down's syndrome. Both studies suggest women with learning disabilities often lacked knowledge and understanding of menstruation and that, as girls, they were not prepared for the onset of menstruation.

At the other end of women's reproductive life cycle, McCarthy's research on menopause (2002) showed similar findings in that many women with learning disabilities were not prepared for the menopause. Although they realised they were experiencing certain physical changes in their bodies they generally lacked awareness as to what these meant. Recent research by Willis (2008) found very similar findings.

In the 21st century it is entirely unnecessary that girls and women with learning disabilities are being left in positions of ignorance about their bodies. It is hard to see a positive side to this and therefore those who care for or work with girls and women with learning disabilities have a responsibility to provide proactive and positive support.

References

Mason L & Cunningham C (2007) An exploration of issues around menstruation for women with Down's syndrome and their carers. *Journal of Applied Research in Intellectual Disabilities* **21** (3) 257–267.

McCarthy M (2002) Going through the menopause: perceptions and experiences of women with intellectual disabilities. *Journal of Intellectual and Developmental Disability* **27** (4) 281–295.

Rodgers J (2001a) The experience and management of menstruation for women with learning disabilities. *Tizard Learning Disability Review* **6** (1) 36–44.

Rodgers J (2001b) Pain, shame, blood and doctors: how women with learning difficulties experience menstruation. *Women's Studies International Forum* **24** (5) 523–539.

Willis D (2008) A decade on: what have we learned about supporting women with intellectual disabilities through the menopause? *Journal of Intellectual Disabilities* **2** (2) 9–23.

Further reading

Cooper E (1999) *Becoming a Woman: A teaching pack on menstruation for people with learning disabilities*. Brighton: Pavilion Publishing.

McCarthy M & Millard L (2003) *Supporting Women with learning disabilities through the menopause: A resource pack*. Brighton: Pavilion Publishing.

Online resources

The Elfrida Society produces a set of accessible booklets on women's reproductive health (periods, fibroids, hysterectomy, etc.) See www.elfrida.com/publications.

You can find a huge range of accessible health information leaflets, including topics on periods and menopause, most of which can be downloaded for free at: www.easyhealth.org.uk.

Chapter 4

Sexuality support for people with profound and multiple disabilities

Angela Mallett and David Stewart

Introduction

'Although we can shape (and mis-shape) sexual expression, sexuality is not an optional extra which we in our wisdom can choose to bestow or withhold according to whether or not some kind of intelligence test is passed.'

(Craft, 1987)

This chapter shares the authors' experience of working with school-aged people with profound learning disabilities. It starts by identifying the different ways in which communication and teaching may take place. It argues that this work is best done in partnership with parents and other carers and suggests a model of 'advocacy groups' to test out ideas about how best to provide support related to sexual issues.

Suggestions are given about what sexual awareness work can be done during personal care and an example is also provided on how to respond to sexual behaviour which is unacceptable in public. There are also examples of other everyday activities to help children and adults with profound learning disabilities learn about their bodies and gender.

Two case studies are referred to throughout to practically illustrate what this might mean in practice.

Case study – Freddie

Freddie is a 45-year-old man with cerebral palsy and profound learning disabilities.

He is handsome with short cropped hair and has a winning smile. He wears trendy clothes and his wheelchair is customised with brightly coloured objects.

Freddie communicates by using a range of facial expressions, but his level of understanding has been difficult to assess. He does, however, laugh at funny jokes and he doesn't laugh at unfunny ones! Full sentences, single words and sensory objects are used as clues to help his understanding.

He is very popular, fun loving, and enjoys activities and being with other people. He has some friends at the residential home where he lives.

One of his main paid carers is a young man called Malcolm. He supports Freddie with his personal and mobility needs.

Freddie uses his right hand very effectively to finger paint and to feel and move objects. With a little guidance he can feed himself with an adapted spoon.

Freddie demonstrates a lack of understanding with regard to inappropriate masturbation. He has never had any sex and relationship education.

Case study – Charlene

Charlene is an 18-year-old woman with profound learning disabilities and she has also been diagnosed as being on the autistic spectrum. She is of African-Caribbean and white British heritage. She has short hair, wears comfortable clothes, but likes wearing pretty clothing.

Charlene communicates by showing emotional responses – she screams and cries when unhappy and laughs when she is happy. Full sentences, single words, photographs and sensory object clues are used to help her understanding. On occasions Charlene will touch requested photographs of everyday objects.

If Charlene is left to her own devices she will sit quietly flapping her hands. It takes a while before Charlene responds to unknown people, but she does respond to known staff and other pupils in her class at school. She has friends in her class.

Charlene lives at home with her mother, who is her main carer looking after all her care needs. Charlene is physically able and she moves around by herself, and when she walks around the school she is guided by an assistant. Charlene can finger feed and is highly motivated to use this skill.

For the last 15 years Charlene has been involved in sexuality and relationship education using the *Bodyworks* (Mallett, 2006) scheme. This has given her practical awareness and an understanding of her body and she has learnt the names of some body parts. With help Charlene has some involvement in the management of her periods and she also has the fullest possible involvement in her self-care. Charlene has enjoyed the activities in *Bodyworks* and she now frequently has a foot massage. She has learnt that she can stop undesired body contact by pushing this away. She knows acceptable social behaviour and with known persons she shows pride in her appearance.

Communication and the understanding of sexual issues

Children and adults with a diagnosis of profound learning disabilities will probably understand a few single spoken words or no spoken language at all. They may, however, be supported to use alternative methods of communication. This is best shown in the following example.

Here are the different ways the idea of 'having a shave' could be communicated:

- ▶ object referenced clue (Park, 2002) – a shaver
- ▶ photograph or picture of a shaver
- ▶ symbol – a line drawing of a shaver
- ▶ tactile clue – a prompt to feel chin
- ▶ smell clue – a smell of aftershave
- ▶ sound clue – the sound of an electric shaver.

Other methods such as taste clues can be used when relevant. It is very important to know the most appropriate and relevant methods of communication for an individual to ensure that the understanding of sexual matters is effective.

Different levels of understanding

With children or adults with profound learning difficulties it is often very difficult to accurately know their level of understanding and there is always the possibility that they may understand everything! Never assume anything, as the following real life situation shows.

Mathew was diagnosed as having profound learning disabilities and it was assumed that he did not understand anything. However, at the age of nine a method of communicating effectively with him was discovered. He is now married, has two children and works in a school as a computer technician. Mathew remembers that people were very disrespectful when he was receiving personal and intimate care.

In Freddie's case study how could it be proved that he really knows the difference between a funny and an unfunny joke?

Explaining sexual issues using different levels

Sexual issues can be explained on three different levels.

1. Everyday spoken language appropriate to the age of the child or adult.
2. Communication at the level for which it has been assumed there is understanding (only when there is clear evidence of understanding at this level will clues at level 3 not be necessary).
3. Full object/sensory clues at the earliest level of understanding.

For example, these three levels can be applied to teaching a girl with profound learning disabilities about having periods before hers start. Here it is assumed that she can recognise objects in life-size photographs.

Level 1

Explain about periods in everyday language and show a video about periods.

Level 2

Prior to her periods starting, demonstrate, and then practice the procedures for managing periods. This may involve the following activities:

- showing a photograph of a sanitary pad to be used as a clue for 'time to change pad'
- practise wearing a sanitary pad
- show a pad with simulated blood
- putting a pad in a bag – with prompts if necessary
- putting the bag in a bin – with prompts if necessary.

This learning will be reinforced by following the above strategies when periods actually begin.

Level 3

Most of the work will need to take place when periods are happening, as it may be likely that the girl is unable to understand the concept of having a period at other times. The tactile and visual clues would be similar to level 2, with the exception of needing to show a pad rather than assuming that a picture will be understood. Attention should also be given to the smell of the items used as there may be a greater ability to recognise and remember objects, activities, or people by smell than through the other senses.

At both level 2 and 3, consideration should be given to the language prompts used. This should be single words to describe objects and actions such as pad, vagina, blood, bag and bin.

Using these three levels promotes opportunities for awareness and understanding to be available to a wide range of children and adults who may have profound learning disabilities.

Expression

In addition to paying detailed attention to the teaching of sexual issues, it is also important to pay attention to what children and adults with profound learning disabilities might be communicating. For example, whenever Freddie's incontinence pad is removed he immediately feels his genital area. He could be communicating:

- ‘What a relief to get that tight pad off’
- ‘It's nice to have a good scratch’
- ‘I like these bits down here – they're only here now and again, so I'd better find out about them before they go again’
- ‘I've got an urgent need to stimulate these parts – it gives me a lovely feeling and makes me feel good’.

When planning responses to communication, careful observation and consideration will need to be given to ensure the most sensitive and appropriate decisions are made. There are usually limited opportunities for people with profound learning disabilities to make choices and decisions, so it is important that whenever possible these are respected.

The involvement of parents, carers and other advocates

A crucial role can be played by parents, carers and other advocates in ensuring that the sexual and relationship needs of children and adults with profound disabilities are met. Here the term advocate is used to include anyone who has an interest in promoting the welfare of a person with profound learning disabilities. This could be a professional advocate, but it could equally be a family friend or staff member who used to work with the person.

It is often difficult for parents to gain knowledge about sexual matters related to children or adults with profound learning disabilities. Ideally parents and other family carers will share their concerns with staff. That is not to say that staff will have the answers, but together the best ways of managing issues of sexuality can be developed.

There are some helpful reading materials for example, *Talking together... About growing up* (Scott and Kerr-Edwards, 2010). Oak Field School in Nottingham has written booklets for parents on a range of issues in relation to sexuality. The two most relevant for parents of children with profound learning disabilities are: *A Planned Dependent Life and Sexuality* and *Your Child's Right*.

Another helpful resource is *Bodyworks* (Mallett, 2006). This is a scheme developed specifically for children and adults with profound learning disabilities and it covers a wide range of sexual and social issues in addition to health, protection, appearance, physical care and independence. There are four sections addressing:

- the head and face
- the hands and arms
- the torso and neck
- the legs and feet.

Each section provides a comprehensive set of frequently asked questions. The authors have found that parents often appreciate discussing sexual issues with other parents of children with profound learning disabilities, as the following quote demonstrates:

> *'I feel comfortable and at ease with other parents – I have learnt a lot from this group, especially from the parents of older children.'*

One benefit is that parents can gain the confidence to talk openly about the sexual issues affecting their child, which is an essential step in gaining support. After all, most people are resistant to talk about sex with anyone other than their partners and most intimate friends.

Making decisions together

Sometimes just one person makes decisions on behalf of a child or adult with profound learning disabilities. Unfortunately, this can inadvertently impose the characteristics of the decision maker onto the child or adult. This can be seen in the two case studies.

Chapter 4 – Sexuality support for people with profound and multiple disabilities

> Charlene's mother Anna is 40 years old. Her choices for Charlene are similar to her own interests. She dresses her in colourful dresses and takes Charlene with her to the local church group where there is lots of singing. At home Charlene spends a lot of time sticking patchwork pieces.
>
> Malcolm is an enthusiastic 24-year-old working with 45-year-old Freddie who has profound learning disabilities. Malcolm's decision-making means that Freddie watches skate boarding, goes to the latest movies and finger paints graffiti designs.

An advocate group can help to ensure that a range of viewpoints are taken into account when choices and decisions are made on behalf of children or adults who are unable to make them for themselves. This includes, but does not need to be limited to areas related to gender and sexual expression.

Advocate groups can consist of a range of different people. For Charlene this may include:

▶ Charlene
▶ her mother Anna
▶ her teacher – a 44-year-old male
▶ a worker from the African-Caribbean club – a 34-year-old female
▶ a 20-year-old female volunteer in the school
▶ a girl who is on the autistic spectrum and has moderate learning disabilities.

If the group are to talk about particularly sensitive or confidential matters the members would be chosen accordingly. For example, it might be decided to exclude men if there is to be a discussion about female masturbation.

Ideally advocate groups meet whenever there are important decisions to be made. However, this is can be unrealistic, as careful planning will be needed to ensure all members are available at the same time. It may, therefore, be necessary to have a regular meeting, for example once a month at a set time.

At advocate groups the person with profound learning disabilities should always be the main focus and communications will be directed towards them.

The other people should give their opinions from the perspective of the child or adult with profound learning disabilities. For example:

'Charlene, I think you would like Mary to be your main care person at school. You seem very comfortable with her and you always smile when you see her.'

At the advocate meetings many decisions can be made such as:

'Who would you like to sit next to in the common room?'

'Do you want to go to the school disco or to the African-Caribbean club?'

'Would you like to go dancing, skating or to the cinema on Thursday nights?'

'Would you like the radio on in the changing area, or do you like it to be quiet?'

Any decisions made by an advocate group will be representative of a range of viewpoints – and it will be less likely to impose one person's values onto the person with profound learning disabilities.

Sexuality awareness during everyday activities

The way support is provided during everyday activities is the most likely way that people with profound learning disabilities will gain an awareness of sexual issues. These should be carefully planned beforehand to ensure maximum benefit.

Personal care time

Personal care time is an ideal time for people to learn about themselves. Appropriately positioned mirrors can help aid the understanding of body parts, body changes and periods. They can also help in the understanding of what the carers are doing during intimate care.

This is can be a rare time for people with profound learning disabilities to explore their bodies if they wish. Carers can involve themselves in tasks such as folding clothing, sorting pads etc. during this time.

It is important, however, to remember that carers should not be exposed to masturbation. One option is to try to provide personal time in the person's bedroom when the person can access their body without the obstacles of incontinence pads. This is not without difficulties; however, careful analysis of the times of bladder and bowel activity can make this possible.

If people are supported to masturbate in the bedroom, there may need to be consideration of whether there are difficulties in reaching an orgasm (see Chapter 2 on Masturbation). The amount of time the person is left alone for may need to be considered in respect of how long it takes to climax.

Public places

Sometimes people with profound learning disabilities will exhibit sexual behaviours in public. This is often because they do not know it is unacceptable. It is the responsibility of others to help them to change such behaviour. In practice this mainly means thinking carefully about how to respond when this happens. This should happen regardless of the possible reason for the behaviour, as Freddie's case study shows.

On outdoor visits Freddie often puts his hands on the bottoms of women who come within his reach. Ideas about why this is happening could include:

- ▶ it could be Freddie's way of saying 'hello'
- ▶ Freddie might think it is funny
- ▶ there could be a sexual motive.

Possible attempts to control this behaviour could be:

- ▶ Freddie being kept 'out of range' of women. This could help him to break the habit.
- ▶ Freddie being given physical prompts to wave to people to say 'hello' and for them to be encouraged to respond in a friendly positive way. This could teach Freddie to say 'hello' to women in an acceptable way.

▶ If Freddie does manage to touch a woman's bottom, give him a clear response that it is unacceptable. Depending on his communication abilities the worker could try to communicate 'that woman is very sad – and I am very sad – we will have to sit quietly for 10 minutes until things feel better'. Alternatively he could be taken immediately home.

Teaching gender and body awareness

Here are some activities which can help people with profound learning disabilities gain a better sense of their own body, including whether they are male or female.

▶ Looking at oneself in a full length mirror. Drawing attention to gender clues is important.

▶ Exploring male and female clothing e.g. sorting clothes to take to a charity shop. This can also help with understanding body shape and size.

▶ Exercises which involve an awareness of other people's bodies. These can include holding and touching others (e.g. during Sherborne's movement sessions (2001) aromatherapy or dancing.)

▶ Anatomically correct models of males and females can be helpful, especially with naming parts.

▶ Life-size models of genitalia can also be used, even though it might be difficult for an individual to associate the models with their own or other people's bodies.

▶ For those people with some understanding of spoken language there are additional exercises in the teaching resource *Living Your life* (Bustard et al, 2010).

When choosing activities or resources it is important to consider age appropriateness. This means paying attention to the stage of an individual's sexual development more than the person's intellectual ability. This may be marked in boys by: the growth of pubic hair, starting to get erections, wet dreams, masturbation and facial hair. In girls this may be shown by: the development of breasts, the start of periods, the growth of pubic hair and masturbation.

While the life expectancy of people with profound learning disabilities is relatively short, there may be a need to attend to sexual changes in the later years – most notably the menopause for women.

Conclusion

Children and adults with profound learning disabilities can, and should, have opportunities to gain awareness and understanding of sexual issues. Most of this work needs to take place as and when sexual situations arise. It can be particularly challenging for staff to do because of the common need for explicitness and repetition.

Every opportunity should be given for the person with profound learning disabilities to be as involved in decision-making as possible. This includes when decisions have to be made by others in their best interests. It has been suggested that advocate groups are a good way of addressing some of the sexual questions which can occur.

References

Bustard S, Corkhill P, Kirby M, Mallett A & Stewart D (2010) *Living Your Life*. London: Brook.

Craft A (1987) *Mental Handicap and Sexuality: Issues for individuals with a mental handicap, their parents and professionals*. Tunbridge Wells: Costello.

Mallett A (2006) *Bodyworks*. Nottingham Oak Field School: Nottingham City Council.

Nottingham Oak Field School (2009) *A Planned Dependent Life and Sexuality*. Nottingham: Nottingham Oak Field School.

Park K (2002) *Objects of Reference in Practice and Theory*. London: Sense.

Scott L & Kerr-Edwards L (2010) *Talking Together … About Growing Up*. London: fpa.

Sherborne V (2001) *Developmental Movement for Children*. London: Worth Publishing.

Further reading

Downs C & Craft A (1997) *Sex in Context*. Brighton: Pavilion Publishing.

Fanstone C & Andrews S (2009) *Learning Disabilities, Sex and the Law*. London: fpa.

Kerr-Edwards L & Scott L (2004) *Talking Together ... About sex and relationships*. London: fpa.

Mencap (2008) *Fact Sheet – PMLD and Sexuality*. London: Mencap.

Park K (2002) *Objects of Reference: Promoting early symbolic communication*. London: RNIB.

Sex Education Forum (2004) Forum Factsheet 32 – Sex and relationships education for children and young people with learning difficulties. London: SEF.

Stewart D (2007) A penis is the man who plays the piano. *SLD Experience Spring* **15–18**.

Chapter 5

Sexual interests, opportunities and choices

David Thompson

Introduction

This chapter looks at three areas of the sexual lives of people with learning disabilities. The first is people's interests and desires to have sex and covers self-stimulation as well as sex and relationships with other people. The second explores the opportunities people have to follow these interests and desires. The third looks at what choices people with learning disabilities have over this area of their lives.

It will show that sexual lives of people with learning disabilities are heavily controlled by a range of factors, most of which individuals have very little control over themselves. Where choice is available it is often very limited, but despite this some people with learning disabilities are taking control over their sexuality and relationships.

Sexual interests

A starting point for this chapter is to recognise that people (whether they have learning disabilities or not) have different hopes for their sexual lives. While society generally suggests an ideal of sex being contained within a loving partnership, this is not what everyone wants. People want and choose different things. This includes:

▶ 'casual' sex with people outside of a relationship

▶ sex with people of the same sex

Chapter 5 – Sexual interests, opportunities and choices

- wanting no sex with other people
- men paying for sex
- women selling sex
- a sexual interest in hurting others
- masturbating to images of children.

You will think that some of the above are acceptable forms of sexual behaviour while others perhaps not. You may also disagree that some of these are 'choices', but are instead the consequence of adverse life events or limited choices. While this may be true for some people, there are definitely individuals who would say each is their free choice.

The point of this introduction is not to shock, but to put the sexual interests of people with learning disabilities in the context of all people's sexual interests. We must be very careful about suggesting that a person with learning disabilities has any particular sexual interests because they have learning disabilities.

There has been a lot of work to try to identify why people have particular sexual interests. For example, psychotherapists have considered how heterosexuality develops, researchers have looked at the balance between nature and nurture for homosexuality, and psychologists have explored the causes of paedophilia (sexual interest in children). A conclusion of this work is that there are a range of factors involved and we can never be sure for any individual why they developed a particular sexual interest.

When working with people with learning disabilities who have a particular sexual interest, trying to explain why this is the case is rarely helpful. There should also be great concern about any attempt to change the sexual interests of a person with learning disabilities – although this is different to trying to control unacceptable sexual behaviour (see Chapter 9).

Trying to change a person's sexual interest generally does not work and the techniques tried are usually unethical. For example, gay men were historically given electric shocks to put them off being sexually interested in men.

What is the interest?

When people have a sexual interest in another person (or persons), they may be interested in:

1. the pleasurable physical sensations that could involve, for example an orgasm, kissing or penetration
2. the meaning of the sexual contact, for example by demonstrating love, a relationship or power
3. the consequences of the sex, for example having children, maintaining a relationship or financial reward.

Our interests in sex with other people are different. For example men are often seen as putting a high value on the physical experience, while women may be more interested in sex as a sign of committed relationship.

These different interests have been found amongst people with learning disabilities. For example, McCarthy's work (1999) with women with learning disabilities showed how the meaning and the consequences of sex were of much more of interest to the women than any sexual pleasure. Indeed many of these women had no concept of sex being physically pleasurable for women (partly because it had never been for them).

Interest in a relationship

People with learning disabilities unsurprisingly want girlfriends, boyfriends or to get married. Like anyone else they may want different things from such a relationship such as:

- companionship
- living and/or sleeping together
- sex
- children
- improved financial situation
- independence from parents or others.

We all live in a society where being in a relationship is expected and so a strong motivation is to fit it. This can be a big factor for some people with learning

disabilities who may see getting or having a relationship as a way of being the same as other people, when society so often focuses on their difference.

Same sex relationships

There should be no surprise that some people with learning disabilities would wish to have relationships or sex with people of the same sex. This can be particularly challenging to those who support people with learning disabilities who find the idea of any relationship difficult. Where people find the confidence to express these desires, too often these are explained away rather than respected. For men with learning disabilities with an interest in men, there are three ways in which this is often done.

▶ The outdated idea that young men go through a 'phase'. The unhidden prejudice being the hope that the men will 'grow out of it'. For men with learning disabilities this hope can extend late into adulthood.

▶ The suggestion that it is a result of men with learning disabilities spending large parts of their lives in same sex environments. This is sometimes called institutional homosexuality and again the motive is to explain away the situation rather than to respect it. With the closure of long stay hospitals there is now less segregation by sex, but the idea is still around. Research has found that men with learning disabilities who previously lived in single sex environments often continued to have sex with men. This was in addition to taking advantage of new opportunities for having sex with women. (Thompson, 2001).

▶ The simplistic assumption that it is a consequence of sexual abuse by men. There is no question about the vulnerability of boys and men with learning disabilities to sexual abuse, but what is questionable is the impact it has on individuals. Suggesting that any man is sexually interested in sex with other men because of experiences of sexual abuse is to over simply the complexity of sexual development. For some people it seems easier to take on this explanation rather than support same sex relationships.

It is worth noting that while ideas have developed to explain why men with learning disabilities are interested in sex with men, this is not matched by a similar concern about why some people with learning disabilities are uninterested in sex – the latter being rarely seen as a problem by carers.

Men and women with learning disabilities being open about same sex interests

In recent years, there have been important developments in equal rights for lesbians and gay men in Britain. This includes equal ages for consent to sexual relationships and the opportunity to enter and end civil partnerships. This does not mean that it is easy for most people to be open about same sex interests. For example, homophobic bullying in schools is widespread and most religions still teach that homosexuality is wrong.

For people with learning disabilities there are additional challenges with aspects of their personal life. This includes their lives generally being heavily scrutinised by carers and lacking the privacy and independence that most adults experience.

There are some people with learning disabilities who are open about wanting relationships with someone of the same sex. Their numbers are however very small, particularly amongst women with learning disabilities. Abbot and Howarth (2005) talked to some of these people and found the following:

▶ most had been bullied and harassed about their sexuality

▶ many wanted support to meet other lesbians and gay men but rarely had the opportunity, and when they did, they often found the gay scene unwelcoming

▶ few had received relevant information from services about sexual issues, however there were isolated examples of some staff doing excellent work in this area.

Despite these experiences, they found a strong desire amongst these women and men to have relationships and to meet other lesbians and gay men.

This means that being serious about supporting different relationships means that it should not be assumed that all people with learning disabilities are heterosexual. It also means recognising that people with other interests will rarely be open about this for fear of the reaction they might get.

One way that services can give a strong message about their respect for different relationships is to support lesbian, gay and bisexual staff to be out at work. This should include being out with service users as well as their colleagues. Where this does not happen, many people with learning disabilities will make assumptions that all staff are in happy heterosexual relationships, when people need to know that the world is more complicated.

Chapter 5 – Sexual interests, opportunities and choices

Sexual identity

Care must be taken separating a person's sexual interests from their sexual identity. This means, for example, not labelling people as lesbian, gay or bisexual, just because a person with learning disabilities is interested in sex with people of the same sex. There are many men who have sex with other men who do not see themselves as either bisexual or gay and would reject being described as such. This is their right, as it is for individuals to decide how they define themselves.

What is important is that people with learning disabilities know the following:

▶ that some people who want relationships with people of the same sex call themselves lesbian, gay or bisexual

▶ that these are not bad names

▶ and they may or may not choose to call themselves as such.

Similarly, where a man with learning disabilities enjoys wearing women's clothes, there should be no rush to label him as, for example, a transvestite. It serves very little purpose.

Fantasy and pornography

Fantasy requires imagination: to think about something that is not happening at that moment. For some people with learning disabilities this could be difficult as it requires abstract thinking. While difficult to prove, research suggests that the greater the cognitive difficulties, the less imagination plays a part in men's sexual lives (Thompson, 2001). Sex, including masturbation, without imagination is a largely physical experience. In contrast, fantasy and imagination play a big part in some people's sex lives. This includes thinking about being with someone attractive (whoever is attractive for the individual), being turned on by particular body parts, clothing or who is in control.

Being sexually attracted to images is an example of sexual fantasy. This includes pop stars in videos, models in magazines and of course pornography. On occasion carers learn that people with learning disabilities (usually men) are aroused by particular images. This should not be a surprise since men (generally) have created a huge pornography industry. What may be different is carers' intimate knowledge of people with learning disabilities' use of

images, because of the access they have to their private lives. Care needs to be taken before suggesting any person with learning disabilities' use of images is 'unusual', because we rarely have similar access to other people's bedside cabinets, for example.

Questions are commonly asked about how to respond to a man with learning disabilities' interest in pornography. These include:

▶ Whether to support men to access it?

▶ Whether to stop men using it?

▶ Where pornography should be kept?

Carers' views about pornography are likely to inform their responses to the above questions. Some feminists are very critical of men's use of pornography, both because of the common exploitation of women who appear in it, and the way it reinforces a view of women as sexual objects. Women with these beliefs are not likely to be supportive of men with learning disabilities having access to pornography. At the other end of the spectrum, some male carers may celebrate its use by men with learning disabilities, and even share their own pornography. This is a very unwise thing to do, as Chapter 1 on the law makes clear.

Although feminist objections to pornography may seem valid and offer a sound argument against its use, it is however unfair to expect men with learning disabilities to be more principled than other men with regard to using pornography. For this reason, perhaps its use should be accepted (although not when it involves people who are not consenting or children). On a practical level, this may mean helping men to understand that it must be used privately and kept away from others. It would be best to avoid supporting men to access pornography with a rare exception maybe if a man is stealing pornography because they lack the ability to access it legally.

Ideally, men with learning disabilities could be helped to understand the problem of pornography for many women. In reality, this is likely to feel like a moral lecture which would make no difference to their behaviour. More useful is to try to help men understand that their experience of sex will not be like that which they see in pornography.

Unusual sexual interests

Partly because of the lack of privacy available to most people with learning disabilities, carers occasionally become aware of unusual sexual interests. This could be for particular objects, fabrics or smells. There should be caution in labelling these as 'strange' and support should focus on ensuring these interests are only pursued in private and safely. As identified above, efforts to change sexual interests are unlikely to be successful.

Opportunities for relationships and sex

Amongst people with learning disabilities the opportunities for relationships and sex vary enormously. There are a wide range of factors involved, only some of which are related to having a learning disability.

Gender

Being a woman or man affects opportunities, whether that is with people of the same and opposite sex. There are very different expectations placed on women and men with regard to relationships and sex. The idea that it is good for men to have lots of partners but bad for women is still very dominant.

In heterosexual sex, the view that men want sex while women concede to have it is a very powerful influence on people's sexual lives. McCarthy (1999) has shown that women with learning disabilities rarely enjoy the physical experience of sex with men and that penetration usually hurts.

The risks of sexual violence and pregnancy can often lead to women with learning disabilities being more protected or supervised than men with similar abilities. This can give women fewer opportunities than men to meet other people and develop relationships.

Physical issues

A number of physical issues can make a big difference. This includes notions of who is attractive and not attractive which affects choices for partners. Physical disability also influences how attractive a person may be perceived to be.

Having a physical disability may impact on a person's opportunities to get out and spend time with people. Common barriers are transport and the accessibility of buildings, including public toilets and other people's homes. There may also be physical difficulties in having sex. In rare cases, people with physical disabilities are given support, for example, to get into a suitable position to have sex.

Physiological issues

Some people with learning disabilities will face physiological barriers to masturbation and sex with other people. This includes difficulties associated with some syndromes, for example, with masturbation for some men with Down's syndrome and Prader-Willi syndrome. It also covers the side effects of medication. Many anti-psychotic and epileptic medicines interfere with the sexual response cycle, though more is known about their effects on men than women.

Degree of learning disability

The extent of a person's learning disability can make a big difference. In reality, people with profound learning disabilities will not be having sex with other people – aside from situations of abuse, from which they should be protected.

A person's relative ability does affect how attractive they may be seen by others. Some people (including people without learning disabilities) would not be attracted to people less able than themselves. Sadly, some less able people will be seen as attractive precisely because of their vulnerability to exploitation.

Many people with learning disabilities understandably seek relationships with people without learning disabilities. The harsh reality is that people without learning disabilities are unlikely to see them as desirable partners, and where relationships do take place the person with learning disabilities is typically exploited sexually and in other ways. Some people with learning disabilities

put up with this exploitation to have a relationship which is valuable to them. For example, Thompson's (2001) research showed that men with learning disabilities who had sex with men who were more able, including those who didn't have learning disabilities, would often have to endure sex that was painful. Usually, this was being penetrated anally without adequate lubrication or a caring partner.

Support of carers

The attitudes of carers, both family carers and paid carers, will make a huge difference to opportunities. Some carers hope that individuals with learning disabilities will benefit from the experiences of relationships, sex and marriage. An example of this shown on a BBC documentary when the mother of Otto Baxter (a young man with Down's syndrome) has been very public about her hopes for her son to have a girlfriend and sex (Otto: Love, Lust and Las Vegas, 2009). It is worth noting that this support rarely extends to the possibilities of same sex relationships or being a parent.

Other carers are much more anxious and take action to prevent intimacy. This includes telling people with learning disabilities to stop touching and to keep away from certain people. Sometimes people are prevented from going to certain places to avoid the risk of relationships developing. One reason many carers are so reluctant for people with learning disabilities to have relationships is their vulnerability to abuse. This is one reason why parents of women with learning disabilities are often more worried about this area of their child's life than the parents of men with learning disabilities. Another reason is the risk of and consequences of pregnancy.

Religion and culture can greatly influence the beliefs of carers, though care needs to be taken not to stereotype people from any particular religions or culture as all holding the same values.

Regardless of carers' attitudes, the availability of practical support can matter a lot. Carers do, for example, influence whether and when a person can go out to meet people. The Stay Up Late campaign (www.stayuplate.org) shows how difficult it can be for the social lives of people with learning disabilities not to be constrained by staff shift patterns. This campaign complains about the common *nights out* for adults with learning disabilities that end prematurely, often at 8pm, because their staff are due to finish their shifts.

Environment and service arrangements

Many people with learning disabilities who lived in large long stay institutions remember the times when there was strict segregation of sexes, not just in the wards themselves, but to the extent that no contact was allowed. The mixing of the sexes came with strong prohibition of any sexual contact including having policies which sanctioned this approach regardless of the consent of the people involved. In spite of this, lots of people were having relationships and sex, which was helped by having so many people living on one site and the low staffing levels. They were largely free from the constraints so many people with learning disabilities face in community settings of close supervision and needing transport to see those people they may be looking to have relationships with.

This is not an argument to return to institutions. A large amount of the sex which was happening was abusive, and there was little dignity or comfort available to people, with no other option but to have sex in dilapidated outbuildings. But it does illustrate how people's opportunities will be dependent on how services are arranged and what transport is available.

It is still the case that people with learning disabilities largely meet potential partners and develop relationships in shared services – whether these be residential, day opportunities or social clubs (see The Specials at www.the-specials.com for an inspiring example of relationships developing in a shared home).

Changes to services inevitably impacts on these opportunities because many people with learning disabilities will be unable to find ways, or get support, to maintain relationships outside of these settings. For example, it is rare for people with learning disabilities living in residential services to have friends rather than relatives visit them – aside from birthday parties.

Increasingly, people with learning disabilities are living by themselves. This does not necessarily mean that they have more opportunities for relationships. It can lead to some people leading very isolated lives with few opportunities to meet people with similar interests, if their support is focused just on the practicalities of life: shopping, cooking, budgeting and cleaning.

Money

We live in a world where people with a lot of money are often deemed attractive. How much money people with learning disabilities have can similarly impact on their relationships and sex. This can work in different ways. A person with learning disabilities who is poor or doesn't have access to their own money may desire or agree to have sex with another person (who may or may not have learning disabilities) partly because they are seen to be relatively rich. This could be just having a few pounds to spend, to having a car or a flat. There are clear risks of exploitation where this is the case.

We also know that there are people who develop relationships with people with learning disabilities to take their benefits. So, for example, a woman with learning disabilities may think she has a boyfriend, when in reality she is being both sexually and financially exploited by a man.

Money can also make a difference as to whether people with learning disabilities can afford clothes that make them feel good or to go out to meet people.

Choices

We have seen that the opportunities that people with learning disabilities have to develop relationships and to have sex are often very limited and controlled by carers. Despite these difficulties many people are making choices in this area of their lives, including the choice not to have intimate relationships. There are many different examples of services providing excellent support in this area of people's lives. These include:

▶ sex and relationship education that talks about how good these things can be as well as the risks

▶ individual carers actively supporting people's opportunities to developing relationships and having sex

▶ dating agencies for people with learning disabilities.

Those people with learning disabilities who get married are amongst the trailblazers in this area, and many of them will have had to overcome a lot of resistance in doing so. So too are those men or women with learning disabilities who come out as lesbian, gay, bisexual or transgendered. To hear about the first people with learning disabilities choosing to enter a civil partnership is something we should all look forward to. Similarly people with learning disabilities getting divorced may provide further evidence of people having greater control over their own lives.

References

Abbot D & Howarth J (2005) *Secret Loves, Hidden Lives: Exploring issues for people with learning difficulties who are gay, lesbian or bisexual.* Bristol: The Policy Press.

BBC3 (2009) *Otto: Love Lust and Las Vegas, 1986.* August 12.

Heavy Load (2010) Stay up late campaign [online]. Available at: http://www.stayuplate.org (accessed July 2010).

McCarthy M (1999) *Sexuality and Women with Learning Disabilities.* London: Jessica Kingsley Publishers.

The Specials (2010) [online]. Available at: http:// www.the-specials.com (accessed July 2010).

Thompson D (2001) Is sex a good thing for men with learning disabilities? *Tizard Learning Disability Review* 6 (1) 4–12.

Further resources

Poole Forum (2010) See it My Way – Relationships. An interactive DVD with people with learning disabilities acting out common relationship situations [online]. Available at: www.pooleforum.co.uk.

SCIE (2010) Working with lesbian, gay, bisexual and transgendered people – people with learning disabilities: Richard's story [online]. Available at www.scie.org.org.uk/sctv.

Chapter 6

Supporting relationships – lessons from what people with learning disabilities have to say

Joan Lesseliers, Geert Van Hove and Tom Van Hoey

Introduction

In the last 15 years or so, people with learning disabilities have begun to be seen in a different light to that of the more distant past: they are now more readily acknowledged to be 'agents' in their own lives. This means seeing individuals as having the ability to understand what is happening around them, to express choices and to initiate change (Kuczynski, 2003). This chapter aims to show how people with learning disabilities seek self-determination within the context of their personal and intimate lives.

This chapter is largely based on the findings of a qualitative study, where people with learning disabilities were asked to speak about various topics relating to personal relationships and sexuality. 46 adults with a wide range of learning disabilities were interviewed; they lived in 24-hour support services in Belgium (see Lesseliers, 1999 for more details.)

This chapter will focus on people with learning disabilities who are seeking or developing relationships. It will discuss how relationships can be supported and cover what some of the risks might be. The chapter uses the words of some people with learning disabilities themselves to demonstrate what they think, how they cope, and how they ultimately hope to change their lives.

The importance of family influence

The view of people with learning disabilities as always being a 'burden' on their families is outdated. Many families value their relative with learning disabilities in terms of his or her positive characteristics and their contribution to the family. Whilst there may be an element of dependency, people with learning disabilities nevertheless contribute to sustaining relationships within the family.

> 'Do you think you take good care of your brothers and sisters?
>
> Yes, I take good care of them
>
> And how do you do that?
>
> They sometimes fight with me and then I say "stop fighting" and they stop. And they tease me, they tease me and then I tease them and so on.'

Parents undoubtedly advise their sons and daughters with learning disabilities about sex and this advice is often aimed at steering them away from sexual relationships. However, what is often overlooked is that 'the child necessarily holds the power to put into action any advice that is offered' (Kuczynski, 2003). In other words, some people with learning disabilities know how to interpret the advice they receive, some think about solutions to overcome obstacles and some know they have to be patient about achieving a greater degree of independence:

> 'Yes, at home I sometimes talk about my girl and about living on my own ... and then my mum says "you've got to ask the manager", I haven't talked about it with the manager.
>
> Why not?
>
> Maybe it's a bit too early.
>
> Yes, later we can, when my mama isn't with me anymore or won't be able to take care of me, yes, then I can sleep with her.'

Key point
▶ It is important to realise the loyalty people with learning disabilities have to their parents, and thus to the norms and values their parents stand for. Working with parents can therefore be an important element for successful sex education with people with learning disabilities.

The importance of staff and service influence

Most residential settings and day services for people with learning disabilities manage friends' access to one another. People with learning disabilities run into all kinds of challenges in developing and maintaining friendships and more intimate relationships, for example:

▶ not being able to invite a friend for a meal at a group home because it would violate fixed amounts of food, or staff rotas, or upset other residents

▶ visits from friends are interrupted by service routines

▶ messages get lost

▶ activities that require transport from staff break down because the staff can't be released from other duties to take them.

The reality is that many people with learning disabilities lead highly scheduled lives and this has an impact on their relationships:

'And you say you don't see [your girlfriend] often?

No

How come?

She goes home every day and I don't, we hardly ever see each other, I do regret that.

It was my darling's birthday the other day

Did you celebrate together?

No, because I wasn't there on Monday, I wasn't there, I was with my mama at home.'

Chapter 6 – Supporting relationships – lessons from what people with learning disabilities have to say

For most people, friendships and relationships emerge among a variety of social relationships, including being part of a family, having a life partner, being a neighbour, being part of a workplace, and being a member of community associations. Many people with learning disabilities often lack these social relationships and the more of these ties and connections a person misses, the fewer opportunities they have to meet and make friends and life partners. The lack of a social network shapes their relationships.

The importance of opportunities for people with learning disabilities to make choices in their homes and day services/workplaces is often overlooked by policy makers, professionals as well as by parents. Moreover, the need to request permission for minor activities has long been recognised as a signifier of low social status (Goffmann, 1961).

Despite many improvements in services over recent decades, it is still the case that for many people with learning disabilities control is exercised over virtually all aspects of their lives. It may appear that in the 21st century, residential settings have more modern policies or enlightened practices; yet when the fundamental nature of those policies and practices are more closely examined, people often remain subject to close supervision. Where this occurs it clearly has a negative impact on their relationships:

> *'You don't caress here?'*
>
> No, I never do, that's impolite, I never do that.
>
> *Not even when you're alone with her?*
>
> No, I always stay in the workshop and when we go for a walk, the educator comes along.
> ___
> *And what about porno films? Do you like that?*
>
> They don't allow us to see that.
> ___
> *Because X [support assistant] always said to me when I feel like [masturbating] I should say so, she said, "always tell us".*
>
> When I do something wrong, with X and I, a remark comes.
>
> *What do they do? What do they say?*
>
> "Don't overdo it".'

Key points

▶ It is important to support people with learning disabilities by offering opportunities to extend their social network and to develop loving relationships.

▶ People with learning disabilities need active support, advice and information, not value judgements about their preferences.

▶ Remember that the more restricted a person's life is, the less likely they are to be able to make, and keep a friendship or relationship. In other words, people cannot be empowered in this one area of life only. It will have a knock-on effect to other aspects of their life.

Building on people's strengths

Despite the many hurdles put in their way, there are people with learning disabilities who form successful and long-term relationships. This research found couples who were aware of each other's limits and respected them. This contributed to the good quality of their relationships. These individuals were able to reflect upon their sexual encounters and often had a positive view of their sexuality. They reported mutual involvement and support of each other's strengths and weaknesses. Given the right support, some people with learning disabilities were able to shape their life as a couple, and saw a future together:

'We are a couple.

And what kind of things do you do as a couple?

Ehm, making plans.'

Key points

▶ Where couples need support and guidance, it is important to support both partners. It may be that one person supports both partners or that each partner has their own support. But providing consistent advice and guidance is important, as well as practical assistance, such as helping them spend private time together.

▶ Some couples only need other people to stop getting their way and can be best supported by being left to get on with it.

Potential problems

Just as with all other people, some people with learning disabilities face difficulties and problems with which they need help. One such problem frequently observed is a pattern of there being different levels of ability between the two partners. In her recent study, Löfgren-Martenson (2004) showed that individuals with moderate disabilities would prefer to be with someone who has mild disabilities. In turn, an individual with mild disabilities would prefer to be with a person without disabilities.

> 'One man is quicker and the other is slower.
>
> *And who is slower, whom do you mean?*
>
> I had a man who was slower than me.
>
> *And do you like it now, the way it is with Y?*
>
> Yes, I do.'

While this can be viewed as understandable, for example, as a strategy to avoid stigmatisation, it can be problematic when it becomes the reality. Marked differences in ability can produce an imbalance of power and thus lead to emotional, physical or sexual abuse. This is especially likely to be the case where the male partner is the more able.

Managing conflict and the difficult emotions that go with that is especially hard when people with learning disabilities are just beginning to form intimate relationships. But it may be equally true for the more experienced, especially those who find it hard to express themselves and cope with distress or anger. Dealing with frustration, disappointment and unanswered questions can be a real challenge and many people with learning disabilities feel that they lack support in dealing with their emotions. However, some will be mature and be measured enough to overcome problems:

> 'Then I picked up the phone and called him myself. I said, "What are we going to do?" So yes, we got together again and left it behind us.'

Others will need help to leave a relationship behind and move on.

Our research, similar to findings of Thompson (1994) and McCarthy (1999) showed that it is not uncommon for some partners to be dominant and others passive in their sexual contact and indeed, their wider lives too. This can lead to some people with learning disabilities not experiencing any real pleasure from sex, but agreeing to it because it is expected of them.

'But did you do that too? Make love to a boy?

Yes

You did? And did you like it?

I didn't like it all that much .... No, but he liked it, and I didn't.'

Whilst this may be a result of the dynamics of the two people involved, environmental issues can also play a big part. For example, if people with learning disabilities have:

▶ insufficient time
▶ lack of privacy
▶ lack of a pleasant environment
▶ concerns about being 'found out'

then their chances of experiencing satisfying and pleasurable feelings from sex are diminished.

'Have you ever made love to a girl naked together in bed, for example?

No, in the toilets at school

And have you entered her with your penis?

No, not that, it didn't work.

Was it too difficult?

Yes.'

Key points

- It is important to work on the self-image of people with learning disabilities in order to make people resilient. Self-esteem can be enhanced through learning about relationships and sex.

- It is important that people understand the difference between failure of a relationship and their failure as a person.

- Offering comfortable circumstances (privacy, time, and accommodation) is also an important condition for fulfilling relationships.

- Abuse, including sexual abuse, within relationships needs to be addressed just as much as abuse from other perpetrators. The abused person may, or may not, wish to be helped to leave the relationship, but should be offered support in any case.

Marriage and parenthood

The wish to get married or to live together in an acknowledged partnership, or to have children, are themes people with learning disabilities often speak about. Clearly it is harder for those in same sex relationships rather than heterosexual ones to speak openly about this, but that does not mean their desires are any less real. Where people with learning disabilities do express these desires explicitly, they often encounter opposition and disapproval from those around them. Although they may wish for it to happen, many do not believe that their future will include a settled and formal partnership.

> *'And why would you like to get married?*
>
> *Because I want to … Y's parents got to agree first, they got to agree and they don't.*
>
> ---
>
> *I would like to but I'm not allowed, aren't I.*
>
> *I'm thirty years old, I should think I'm allowed to do more.'*

Particularly when it comes to having children, many are resigned to their 'fate', i.e. that they will never have children. Some women especially undergo sterilisation or are put on contraception for the whole of their reproductive lives. In many cases this happens without informed consent, sometimes with little or no prior information, causing a lot of grief in the long term. Many people

with learning disabilities can point to the large differences between their life and that of their brothers and sisters. When it comes to the very big decisions in life, many people with learning disabilities seem to be rendered powerless:

'What do you feel about it, psychologically, in your head, how does it feel to be sterilised?

Well, how does it feel, lousy.

Why?

Because my sister can get children and I can't, because she can get married and I can't.'

Key points

▶ It is important to discuss with people with learning disabilities their wishes for their future lives.

▶ Where people can be helped to form long-term partnerships, either heterosexual or same sex, they should be helped to do so, i.e. all unnecessary obstacles need to be removed. For example, if people believe it is against the law for them to get married, they need to be properly informed.

▶ Where the obstacles are real, then people need to be supported to either overcome them and possibly suffer the consequences, e.g. go against their parents' wishes and risk losing their relationship with them, or to come to terms with the situation.

▶ Where people are denied what they really want in life, this can have long term implications for their mental health. Many people with learning disabilities carry a lot a grief for many years and this should be acknowledged, not ignored.

Conclusion

On the one hand, we can say that the experiences of people with learning disabilities are as broad as other people's: some people are in love, some are not; some have many friends, others don't etc. But it is also true to say that the personal and intimate lives of people with learning disabilities are generally quite different from most other adults and this chapter has tried to show the ways in which these differences arise, as well as give some ideas for overcoming some of the obstacles.

For those who support people with learning disabilities, the key to success is to intervene in a way which maximises the individual's control and choices in their own life, without being over-demanding. Listening to what people really want and supporting a network which allows people to meet friends and lovers in a more natural way are two of the most effective ways to initiate change. Offering positive life experiences in terms of relationship support means improving the general quality of people's lives. When given sufficient opportunities, people with learning disabilities are often as able as other people to show commitment, mutual support, friendship and love.

References

Goffmann E (1961) *Asylums: Essays on the social situation of mental patients and other inmates.* Harmondsworth Middlesex: Penguin Books.

Kuczynski L (Ed) (2003) *Handbook of Dynamics in Parent-Child Relations.* Thousand Oaks. CA: Sage.

Lesseliers J (1999) A right to sexuality? *British Journal of Learning Disabilities* **27** (4) 137–140.

Löfgren-Martenson L (2004) "May I?" About sexuality and love in the new generation with intellectual disabilities. *Disability and Society* **22** (3) 197–207.

McCarthy M (1999) *Sexuality and Women with Learning Disabilities.* London: Jessica Kingsley Publishers.

Thompson D (1994) Sexual experiences and sexual identity for men with learning disabilities who have sex with men. *Changes* **12** (4) 255–263

Chapter 7

Pregnancy, contraception and women choosing to have a child

Sandra Baum and Natasha Alexander

Introduction

This chapter assumes that people with learning disabilities can consent to pregnancy and have the capacity to do this, and that the woman with learning disabilities has engaged in sexual intercourse with a man. Single women or women in relationships may need an advocate to help them voice their wishes and rights to have a baby. Women with learning disabilities in same sex relationships may have further battles to face if, for example, they need to be referred for fertility treatment with the use of donor sperm. This chapter has five sections:

- Attitudes towards women with learning disabilities becoming pregnant
- Contraception
- Planning to get pregnant
- Having a baby
- Supporting parenting skills

Attitudes to women with learning disabilities becoming pregnant

Key points
- ▶ The possibility of pregnancy often raises fierce debate and controversy.
- ▶ It is frequently assumed that people with learning disabilities will be poor parents.
- ▶ 40%–60% of children are removed from parents with learning disabilities.
- ▶ However, people with learning disabilities can be good parents and can improve their skills.
- ▶ Pregnancy will be marked by assessment, criticism, change and judgment.

Historically there have been long-standing concerns about people with learning disabilities becoming parents. Two contradictory beliefs in the late 19th and early 20th centuries coloured people's attitudes, and these were that people with learning disabilities were either considered child-like and asexual or promiscuous, immoral and a sexual threat to others. This latter idea led to people with learning disabilities being routinely institutionalised and segregated to prevent reproduction, and subjected to enforced sterilisation. These beliefs, both stigmatising and negative, have left a long-standing legacy and today parenting is still considered an undesirable option and something to be avoided. The possibility of women with learning disabilities becoming pregnant in the 21st century evokes a variety of responses from professionals and carers, often triggering debate and controversy.

The debate reflects the fact that many research studies have shown that parents with learning disabilities are more likely to live in poverty, be isolated, victimised, have poor models of parenting, difficult relationship histories and increased psychological distress, all of which will affect their ability to cope with the demands of raising children. However, by contrast, research has also found that parents with learning disabilities can attend to the physical needs of their children, give them love and affection, and improve their parenting skills with training (McGaw, 1998). Sadly, the research shows too, that between 40–60% of children are removed from parents with learning disabilities and there is a 10% chance of children being removed

immediately after birth. Child protection proceedings are prone to rapid decisions. Research has shown that the removal of children may be viewed as a consequence of poor parenting or because it is assumed that people with learning disabilities will neglect their children without any evidence suggesting that this is the case. In fact if there is neglect, it is more likely to be due to poor professional practice, services or supports (Booth & Booth 1994). Another assumption is that women with learning disabilities will have children who will also have learning disabilities, which is also not necessarily the case.

Between 60–90% of women with mild learning disabilities want to marry and have children (Bratlinger 1985, cited in Aunos & Feldman, 2002). Some of the rewards of parenthood for people with learning disabilities are that it raises their self-esteem, they feel personally fulfilled, and it increases the sense of identification with other parents and gives opportunities for loving relationships. Parenthood is something that people accomplish for themselves in the face of opposition from others. However, carers' own beliefs and attitudes can play a major role in effecting choices of people with learning disabilities, and if a woman with learning disabilities does get pregnant, she will frequently face assessment, criticism, change and judgment.

Contraception

Key points

- ▶ Women with learning disabilities have a right to choose and use contraception.

- ▶ Depo-Provera is over-used.

- ▶ Women with learning disabilities have little knowledge about contraception and tend to rely on others to make decisions for them.

- ▶ Women with learning disabilities need to be given accessible information to make informed choices about which option they prefer.

- ▶ Women with learning disabilities need to be supported to attend medical appointments with female support workers.

- ▶ A capacity assessment to ensure consent should be conducted.

Chapter 7 – Pregnancy, contraception and women choosing to have a child

Contraception is available for women with learning disabilities who want to avoid unwanted pregnancies in the same way as it is for other women of child-bearing age. However, research has shown that patterns of contraceptive use by women with learning disabilities do not match those of other women of child-bearing age (McCarthy, 2009). Depo-Provera is far more likely to be used by women with learning disabilities. The use of barrier methods is very uncommon but the use of the Pill is common as it is for other women in the general population. It is also known that although the Pill is used to stop unwanted pregnancies for women with learning disabilities, it is also used to manage menstrual problems and in some cases when women with learning disabilities are not sexually active and do not have menstrual problems, it is used 'just in case' (McCarthy, 2009). The research shows that women with learning disabilities have little knowledge about contraception and tend to rely on others such as general practitioners (GPs) and their support workers to make decisions for them. They rarely ask questions to the GP, and tend not to remember if the GP has asked them anything either. There are many ways that this situation can be improved as the following discussion illustrates.

The best way to support women with learning disabilities to avoid an unwanted pregnancy is for them to receive accessible information about contraception so that they can make informed choices about which option they prefer, though clearly cultural and religious issues will need to be taken into account. This work is best done by a female support worker/carer or community nurse from the local community learning disabilities team before meeting the GP or health care professional. Women with learning disabilities tend to have a general lack of knowledge about contraception and reproduction, and so it is important to remember this even if they appear to be very able and independent. Many women do not know the link between fertility and the need for contraception, in that sex is necessary for pregnancy, or that the menopause marks the end of fertility.

It is important to work collaboratively with women with learning disabilities to ascertain what information they need and in which format it is most easily understood. They will require information about what the different choices are, how they work, how they are used, any side effects, and the advantages and disadvantages of each type of contraception. Accessible information includes the use of visual aids such as pictures, photographs and drawings to aid understanding. The FPA has a variety of relevant materials and local family planning clinics may also be able to help. It is important not to make assumptions about levels of comprehension and to always ask the woman with learning disabilities to repeat what is being talked about in order to check understanding.

When attending medical appointments to discuss contraception, women with learning disabilities have said that they prefer being with a female support worker or carer and, if possible, prefer to see a female doctor. It is imperative that women with learning disabilities decide themselves about whether to have contraception or not, and how long to use it for, and also that they be given information about when to cease using it. The test of capacity from the Mental Capacity Act (2005) (Department of Constitutional Affairs, 2007) can help the GP or family planning professional with this task by checking with the woman with learning disabilities that:

- they understand the decision they have to make
- they understand the consequences of making or not making the decision
- they can retain the information, and weigh it up
- they can communicate their decision.

The support worker or carer can aid the woman with learning disabilities and the GP in this process by taking visual aids to the consultation, encouraging the woman with learning disabilities to speak to the GP, and preparing simple questions in advance to facilitate communication.

Planning to get pregnant

Key points

- There are limited available resources for supporting women with learning disabilities who plan to get pregnant, whether they are single or in a relationship.

- Women with learning disabilities may not feel supported in their decision to start a family. Professionals who do support them may feel isolated if other professionals think that it is a bad idea.

- It is useful for an advocate to be involved in supporting the woman or couple so as to voice her wishes and rights to start a family.

- Multi-disciplinary joint working may be needed, for example, if there are ethical dilemmas around genetic factors or medication.

The available literature and resources are limited concerning women with learning disabilities who plan to get pregnant. CHANGE has published accessible resources targeted at heterosexual couples such as *Planning a Baby*, which is useful for supporting women with their decision to get pregnant and includes practical advice about nutrition, coming off contraception, monitoring one's menstrual cycle and looking out for indications of ovulation. This resource also acknowledges that it can be hard for women with learning disabilities to decide to have a baby 'because other people like social workers, doctors or parents might not think it is a good idea' (2010). The booklet advises that the potential mother-to-be considers what support she might need, and talks it over with someone she trusts.

Supporting a woman with learning disabilities may be straightforward or complicated, depending on the particular circumstances. For example, there may be dilemmas regarding genetic factors or she may be on medication that interferes with her ability to become pregnant, in which case her GP or psychiatrist will need to advise about the way to go forward. It is important that support is provided in an accessible way, as women with learning disabilities may not be able to access the resources that women without learning disabilities use to learn about increasing their fertility and getting pregnant, such as magazines, books and workshops.

Having a baby

Key points
▶ Pregnant women with learning disabilities may present late to services and may therefore miss out on early antenatal care.

▶ Services should ensure that advice and information given to women is accessible, provided in different formats, and time should be given to ensure that the woman understands.

▶ Assessment of needs should be undertaken as soon as the pregnancy is identified.

▶ Assumptions about a lack of parental competency should not be made purely because the parent-to-be has learning disabilities.

The existing literature on parents with learning disabilities focuses on supporting women once they are pregnant. Little relates to the support of single women or couples with learning disabilities in planning to have a baby. This section will discuss issues relating to both of these groups.

Anecdotal evidence indicates that women with learning disabilities may present late to services, when they are several months pregnant. This may be because they are frightened that their children may be taken away from them, or because of a lack of awareness or acknowledgement of their condition. Some women may not be aware of the services available to them, or of the need to inform the health services that they are pregnant. This may result in women missing out on early antenatal care and support.

There are many policy documents, protocols and organisations that provide guidance on supporting parents with learning disabilities. *The Good Practice Guidelines on Working with Parents with a Learning Disability* (Department of Health & Department for Education and Skills, 2007) states that services should make 'reasonable adjustments' to ensure that provision is accessible and suitable for people with learning disabilities. This means that once a woman with learning disabilities has discovered that she is pregnant, like anyone else, she should receive services from mainstream antenatal services including GPs and midwives.

The guidelines also advise that referrals should be made to community learning disability teams (CLDT), unless there are additional child welfare concerns, for example, if the woman already has children, in which case a referral should also be made to children's services. In addition, specialist midwives may be involved if there are concerns about the safety of the unborn baby. CLDTs are well placed to advise on the development of accessible information about pregnancy, antenatal care and preparing for parenthood, and may also undertake assessments and make recommendations for support.

Information

Information for parents and parents-to-be with learning disabilities should be made accessible. It is advisable to allow lots of time to go through the information in detail and discuss with parents and parents-to-be how they can apply the advice to their own situation. Accessible information may include easy-read versions of leaflets.

Assessment

The guidelines advise that identification of needs should start when the pregnancy is confirmed. Adult learning disability services and children's services need to work together to make sure that they have agreed referral procedures, and that they are working in partnership to meet the needs of both the parents with learning disabilities and their children.

Some mothers with learning disabilities manage very well, while others have particular difficulties. It is important that those working with parents do not automatically assume that the difficulties are due to the learning disabilities, as they may be due to other factors such as poor experiences in childhood, inadequate social support networks, inadequate home environments, stress, poverty, relationship difficulties or financial difficulties.

Assessments undertaken by adult CLDTs may include the following.

- Psychometric assessments
    - Does the mother-to-be have learning disabilities?
    - To what extent do her learning disabilities impact on her general level of functioning and her ability to parent her child?
    - What sort of support is she likely to need in order to learn new tasks, develop an understanding, and increase her confidence and experiences in order to meet the needs of her child?

It should be noted that having learning disabilities does not mean that the person cannot learn new skills; nor does it mean that the person will not be able to look after their child. Psychometric assessments are useful, but should not be relied on solely as an indication of parenting ability.

- *Parenting Assessment Manual* (PAM) (McGaw *et al*, 1999; 2007). This is the most common tool that support workers, health and social services professionals use to assess the parental knowledge, skills and practice of people with learning disabilities. It is preferable to carry out this assessment in conjunction with children's services where possible.

Supporting parenting skills

Key points

- People working with parents-to-be who have learning disabilities need to spend time ensuring that they understand information given to them.
- There are many different ways of supporting people to develop parenting skills.
- It is natural for all new parents to feel anxious and worried about their parenting skills and this should be considered when working with parents with learning disabilities.

Table 7.1 (on p120) gives examples of difficulties that may be faced by parents-to-be with ideas for support.

Conclusion

Attitudes towards people with learning disabilities forming sexual relationships and becoming parents are becoming more positive. There is increasing acknowledgement and support of their right to bring up families of their own. Unfortunately, despite changing attitudes and an increase in services and resources, people with learning disabilities still do not seem to have the same access as people without learning disabilities to a wide range of contraception choices, access to support to become pregnant, or support to keep their children once they do have them. The area is still fraught with controversy and debate about whether people with learning disabilities make good enough parents. Clearly the appropriate level of support is crucial, and money and services need to be available to ensure that parents with learning disabilities get needs-led, rather than resource-led support. Mainstream services have an obligation to ensure that information is given in an accessible way and that people with learning disabilities are fully involved with any decisions that are made. Children and adult learning disabilities services are working more in partnership with each other but there is still a long way to go.

Table 7.1:

Examples of difficulties parents-to-be may face	Support required
Finding it difficult to learn new skills or understand new or complex information.	Allow plenty of time. Show the person how to carry out the task or skill several times. Provide accessible information in a medium that fits with how the parent learns best e.g. pictures, or DVD.
Finding it difficult to retain the knowledge and skills they have learned.	Memory aids (e.g. pictorial prompts around the home) and having lots of opportunities to practice new skills with support can help maintain learning. Ask the person to repeat what is being asked in order to check they have understood.
Finding it hard to generalise skills to different situations.	Opportunities to practice new skills in various contexts.
Difficulty following meetings and lacking in confidence to voice their opinion.	An advocate may be useful to help explain the process of meetings and what is being discussed, as well as being able to support the person with learning disabilities to voice their opinion.

Case study

Mrs B has moderate learning disabilities. She recently got married in Bangladesh and when she returned with her husband who does not have learning disabilities, she was a few months pregnant. She lives with her husband, her brother and her sister-in-law.

She went to see her GP with her sister-in-law who asked Mrs B some questions to find out about her knowledge of the pregnancy. Mrs B was then referred to antenatal and midwifery services, informing them that she had

learning disabilities. Following a detailed assessment by the midwife, she was referred to the social work department at the local general hospital who arranged a pre-birth conference and invited the community nurse from the adult learning disabilities team to attend.

At that meeting it was decided that the community nurse would assess Mrs B's knowledge of childcare and parenting skills, using sections of the *PAM* (McGaw *et al*, 2007). It was highlighted that she had a number of needs and would require support with her parenting. She was offered an advocate and was given, *You & Your Baby 0–1 year* (CHANGE, 2010). The family was supportive and helped her to understand the skills she had to learn.

After the baby was born, the children in need social work team were informed and a further assessment took place with a social worker from the adult learning disabilities team. The baby was discharged home under the care of the husband, brother and sister-in-law, and further assessments took place for all family members by the health visitor and the children in need team. A child protection conference took place and the baby was subject to a child protection plan. At the child protection review meeting the health visitor and the children in need team reported that the baby was well looked after and that the family had co-operated well with child services. They made sure that Mrs B was not left unsupervised with the baby but that she should carry out all practical tasks including feeding and changing the baby. The baby was taken off the protection plan and was supported by Mrs B's social worker and the community nurse. Mrs B and her husband also were referred to Sure Start[1] and the family continue to be monitored.

---

[1] Sure Start was a New Labour government initiative to deliver the best start in life for every child by bringing together early education, childcare, health and family support.

References

Aunos M & Feldman MA (2002) Attitudes towards sexuality, sterilisation and parenting rights of persons with intellectual disabilities. *Journal of Applied Research in Intellectual Disabilities* **15** 285–296.

Bratlinger EA (1985) Mildly mentally retarded secondary students' information about sexual and attitudes toward sexuality and sexuality education. *Education and Training of the Mentally Retarded* **20** 99–108.

Booth T & Booth W (1994) *Parenting Under Pressure: Mothers and fathers with learning difficulties*. Buckingham: Open University Press.

CHANGE (2010) *You and Your Baby 0–1 year* [online]. Available at: www.changepeople.co.uk (accessed July 2010).

Department of Constitutional Affairs (2007) *Mental Capacity Act (2005) Code of Practice*. London: TSO.

Department of Health & Department for Education and Skills (2007) *Good practice guidance on working with parents with a learning disability*. London: HMSO.

McCarthy M (2009) I have the jab so I can't be blamed for getting pregnant: contraception and women with learning disabilities. *Women's Studies International Forum* **32** 198–208.

McGaw S (1998) Practical support for parents with learning disabilities. In: J O'Hara & A Sperlinger (Eds) *Adults with Learning Disabilities* **123–8**. New York: Wiley.

McGaw S, Beckley K, Connolly C & Ball K (1999) *Parent Assessment Manual*. Truro: Trecare NHS Trust.

McGaw S, Beckley K, Connolly C & Ball K (2007) *Parent Assessment Manual (Second edition)*. Truro: Pill Creek Publishing.

Resources

FPA [online]. Available at: www.fpa.org.uk (accessed July 2010).

CHANGE (2010) *You and Your Baby 0–1 year* [online]. Available at: www.changepeople.co.uk (accessed July 2010).

CHANGE (2010) *You and Your Little Child 1–5* [online]. Available at: www.changepeople.co.uk (accessed July 2010).

CHANGE (2010) *You and Your Little Child 1–5* [online]. Available at: www.changepeople.co.uk (accessed July 2010).

CHANGE (2010) *Planning a Baby* [online]. Available at: www.changepeople.co.uk (accessed July 2010).

CHANGE (2010) *My Pregnancy, My Choice* [online]. Available at: www.changepeople.co.uk (accessed July 2010).

Chapter 8

Concerns about people with learning disabilities being sexually abused

Deborah Kitson

Introduction

'Any form of sexual activity that's against your will constitutes as sexual abuse. This includes bodily contact (such as sexual kissing, touching, fondling of genitals or penetration – oral, anal or vaginal) and genital exposure (flashing) verbal pressure for sex and sexual exploitation through pornography or prostitution'

(Thesite.org, 2010)

This chapter looks at what is known about the sexual abuse of people with learning disabilities; how it is identified that a person has been abused; what action can be taken and the support that should be considered for the victims of sexual abuse. It will look at relevant government initiatives that have impacted on this work and how the justice system deals with victims and witnesses with learning disabilities. Reference will also be made to specific areas of concern that have recently been highlighted including the forced marriage of people with learning disabilities and the risks posed by internet sites.

Background

One has only to go back to the 1970s and 80s to find evidence that people with learning disabilities were disregarded as sexual beings and subsequently their sexual needs were ignored. Many grew up without any formal or informal sex education and as a result were both denied their right to develop appropriate and consenting relationships and left vulnerable to abuse. Most people gain their sexual knowledge in a variety of ways – in the classroom, from family, parents and siblings, from the media and perhaps most significantly from sharing our thoughts and feelings with peers and from sexual experimentation.

This was not so for people with learning disabilities who received little in the way of formal sex education in school, were for the most part were protected by friends and family and were often not allowed the independence to learn from peers, as 'bike

shed' experiences were off limits. Such approaches were shaped by a fear that to give knowledge would not only encourage sexual activity, but thereby increase the risk of abuse. In reality, ignorance is no protection, and a lack of sexual knowledge increases vulnerability to abuse. Limitations in sexual knowledge may lead to people with learning disabilities not understanding risks, not complaining when they have been abused and consequently becoming easy targets for perpetrators.

Ann Craft and others pioneered the work in the 70s looking at the fundamental rights of people with learning disabilities to have their sexuality recognised and acknowledged:

> *'To be a human being is to be a sexual being. Although there may be a range of intensity varying over time, we all have sexual needs, feelings and drives from the most profoundly handicapped to the most able among us. Although we can shape (and misshape) sexual expression, sexuality is not an optional extra which we in our wisdom can choose to bestow or withhold according to whether or not some kind of intelligence test is passed.'*
>
> (Craft, 1987)

A shift in thinking encouraged by pioneers in this field forced services to also address the vulnerability of people with learning disabilities. The need to look at these issues was further reinforced by the advent of community care, the concept of normalisation and the slow and planned closure of many of the large institutions. In the late 80s, Craft and others recognised that while sexuality and sexual abuse should not be treated as one and the same, there was a need to acknowledge that people with learning disabilities could only have fulfilling sexual experiences and relationships if they had the capacity to consent and were also able to protect themselves from unwanted sexual encounters. It was recognised that staff needed guidelines to work within, both for safeguarding the people they were supporting and for their own professional protection. So policies began to be developed nationally and pockets of good practice developed. Before this time when the sexuality of people with learning disabilities was largely being ignored, many people with learning disabilities were victims of sexual abuse and today still hold memories of the experiences of abuse that they suffered at that time. Evidence has since come to light to reveal that there was widespread abuse within hospital and residential settings, where the majority of people were being cared for outside the family home. The contraceptive Pill was prescribed widely for women with learning disabilities under the guise of helping with the management of periods, but this, notwithstanding the inherent risks of being on the Pill long term, also managed

to veil the reality of what was happening. People with learning disabilities so often depend on others raising concerns on their behalf and together faced with a culture that denied the possibility of abuse, it was allowed to thrive.

Although the sexual abuse of children was highlighted in the 1980s, Cooke's research in 2000 demonstrated that the sexuality of people with learning disabilities was continuing to be ignored. Her research revealed that where there was a child protection issue in a family it was not uncommon for services to fail to realise that the disabled child was also at risk as well as their siblings. This represents poor practice on a number of levels including a lack of understanding about the behaviour and motive of the abuser but it was also clearly a denial of the sexuality and subsequent vulnerability of the disabled child. In her research she refers frequently to the disabled child being differently treated to other children – signs of abuse were ignored and disclosures viewed as fabrications. The necessary care and support that the abused child required was not available to the disabled child inferring a further assumption that firstly the disabled child would not be able to respond to, for example, therapeutic input and post-abuse treatment but that these were not as necessary where the child had a disability. In summary, this research suggested that:

▶ children with disabilities are more likely to be abused

▶ child protection systems do not address the specific needs of disabled children

▶ disabled children do not have equal access to therapeutic interventions

▶ they do not have equal access to justice.

Despite recent initiatives to address these concerns including the campaigning group Every Disabled Child Matters, *Working Together to Safeguard Children* (2010) and the recent multi-agency practice guidance, the situation has been slow to change and the specific needs of disabled children continue to be overlooked.

Brown and Turk in the 90s carried out some ground-breaking research looking at the sexual abuse of adults with learning disabilities (1993). They refer to statistics in this research and although the authors suggest that they were probably only seeing the 'tip of the iceberg' these figures were useful in that they showed that sexual abuse does happen and has to be addressed. At the time of their research many professionals and others were still denying that there was a problem – people might acknowledge that it could occur but certainly not where they were working – people were still hoping to avoid what

was clearly, to many, an unpleasant reality. 'The extent of physical and sexual abuse of mentally handicapped adults will probably never be known, but the first academic research suggests there are 1,400 cases of sexual abuse reported to the authorities every year.' (Brown *et al*, 2005)

Vulnerabilities

Children and adults with learning disabilities may be more vulnerable than others for a number of reasons including:

- lack of knowledge and information
- feeling of disempowerment
- need for personal intimate care
- poor verbal communication and alternative methods of communication
- cared for by numbers of carers in different environments
- not being believed or listened to
- limited understanding to enable them to understand risk
- unaware of complaints procedures and the right to complain.

Services can also add to the vulnerability of the people they support with:

- closed cultures that fail to report abuse
- negative attitudes and assumptions about the sexuality of people with learning disabilities
- inadequacies in service provision
- ineffective multi-agency working
- poor policies and staff training.

Consent and capacity

Whilst a child, with or without learning disabilities, cannot consent to sexual activity, the situation for adults with a learning disability is more complex (see Chapter 1). Practitioners need to balance the requirement to protect a

potentially vulnerable individual from abuse with the recognition that they have a right to be sexually active. In order to consent to sexual activity, a person must be able to understand what it is they are consenting to and the likely consequences of any action or inaction:

> 'A person consents if he agrees by choice and has the freedom and capacity to make that choice' (Section 74, Sexual Offences Act, 2003).

Consent is central to many of the difficulties that arise when dealing with an incident of alleged abuse, or when discussing a developing sexual relationship between two people with learning disabilities. When someone is unable to communicate clearly or when they only have limited understanding of a situation, the task of assessing whether or not they have given consent is fraught with dilemmas. If they are consenting to sexual activity, but carers misunderstand and act to stop the contact, the adults' right to have a sexual relationship has been denied. On the other hand, if no one steps in and the act was not consensual, then sexual abuse could continue.

Nothing in the Mental Capacity Act (2005) covering England and Wales permits a decision to be made on someone else's behalf on issues relating to consent to marriage or a civil partnership, consent to have sexual relations, consent to divorce or dissolution of a civil partnership. Case law has established that the individual must have sufficient understanding of the sexual nature and character of the act of sexual intercourse, and of the reasonably foreseeable consequence of sexual intercourse to have the capacity to choose whether or not to engage in it. The individual will need to have the capacity to decide whether to give or withhold consent to sexual intercourse and to communicate their choice to their partner (Local Authority X v MM and KM [2007] EWHC 2689 (Fam)(16 November 2007)).

Signs and signals of sexual abuse

There is a wide range of indicators that staff need to be aware of that might indicate possible sexual abuse. It is useful to consider these signs in four categories: medical, forensic, behavioural/emotional or circumstantial (Brown & Craft, 1992). It is our responsibility to record these signs and report our concerns.

Belle case study part 1

Belle lives in a residential school but spends occasional weekends at home. She has been at the school for three years and had appeared to be well settled. She is popular with staff and her peers, but staff at the school have been concerned that she seems to have changed recently and is often agitated. More recently she has also been displaying sexualised behaviour including masturbating and appears to be very distressed about this. A decision has been taken to report their concerns.

Everyone uses alternative methods of communication to interact and to let people know how they feel. Many people with learning disabilities will be unable to say that they have been sexually abused. They may not be able to communicate verbally, may not understand what has occurred, may accept the situation as 'normal' or may not understand that they have a right to complain. Some people's feelings may only be communicated through their behaviour and so there is a need to be aware, not only of the signs and signals that may indicate abuse, but also how to interpret these signs. Interpretation is fraught with difficulties as there might be innocent explanations to the indicators that cause concern, for example, crying when a member of staff takes her to the toilet could indicate that the person is frightened of the member of staff or of something unpleasant that has occurred in the toilet area. On the other hand, it may indicate that they have a medical problem for example a urinary tract infection or that they are unhappy about interrupting their current activity. For these reasons, it is important to observe changes, consider and record them, but not to make assumptions about their cause.

Belle case study part 2

The concerns about Belle were reported to the adult care team. When the social worker visited she spoke to the staff and referred to the records. She noticed that detailed records had been kept and they revealed that these agitated states had occurred every Friday over the past few months and the sexualised behaviour only seemed to occur on Mondays, but not every week. She decided that the situation should be explored further and so she referred the concerns to the safeguarding team for further investigation.

Who abuses?

There are many assumptions about who abuses but the simple fact is that anyone might be an abuser. To believe these common assumptions may result in us failing to acknowledge the abuse. While Turk and Brown (1993) showed that in their study the majority of known perpetrators were men, it should not be assumed that women never abuse. People with learning disabilities themselves may be perpetrators.

Cooke's research showed that in a significant minority of cases adolescents with learning disabilities who had themselves been abused were going on to sexually abuse other children (2000). This unexpected finding led to the research by Rachel Fyson looking at *Young People with Learning Disabilities who Show Sexually Inappropriate or Abusive Behaviours* (2005). Her work shows that there are many reasons why people with learning disabilities abuse. These include there being fewer interventions than with non-learning disabled children when inappropriate behaviour is witnessed. For example, there can be a reluctance to look beyond the disability and to respond to the behaviour, reticence about referring to appropriate agencies, and difficulties of agencies, working together.

Responding to disclosures, allegations and suspicion of sexual abuse

Recognition of the sexual abuse of adults has come on the back of the work that has been done with children. *No Secrets* (2000) covered England and recommended that areas developed and implemented safeguarding procedures. Since then, adult safeguarding boards, safeguarding teams and safeguarding leads in statutory and independent and voluntary sectors have been established. At time of writing, it is unknown the extent to which the recent review will lead to adult protection legislation which could place a statutory requirement on this work.

There has also been further work with regard to safeguarding children following a number of high-profile cases. The recent *Working Together to Safeguard Children* (2010) sets out how individuals and organisations should work together to safeguard and promote the welfare of children. Progress has been made in the last 10 years and a number of pieces of legislation and government initiatives have contributed to this (see **table 8.1**).

Table 8.1: Recent laws and government policies

Speaking Up For Justice (1998)

A report of the Interdepartmental Working Group on the treatment of vulnerable or intimidated witnesses in the Criminal Justice System made a total of 78 recommendations for improvements to the criminal justice system for vulnerable or intimidated witnesses including children.

No Secrets (2000) (England)/In Safe Hands (2002) (Wales)

Guidance on developing and implementing multi-agency policies and procedures to protect vulnerable adults from abuse. Gave local authorities a responsibility to co-ordinate action when a vulnerable adult is believed to be suffering abuse.

Achieving Best Evidence (2000 & 2007)

A document that offers guidance for vulnerable or intimidated witnesses including children. They replaced the previous Memorandum of Good Practice and covers the planning and conducting of interviews, witness preparation and support.

Sexual Offences Laws

The Sexual Offences Act (2003), Sexual Offences (Northern Ireland) Order (2008) and Sexual Offences (Scotland) Act (2009) have introduced a number of new offences concerning vulnerable adults and children across the UK (see Chapter 1).

The Mental Capacity Act (2005)

Its general principle is that everybody has capacity unless it is proved otherwise and that they should be supported to make their own decisions. Anything done for or on behalf of people without capacity to make a specific decision must be in their best interests. As part of this, consideration needs to be given to minimising restriction placed upon them.

Safeguarding Vulnerable Groups Act (2006)

Introduced by this act, the Independent Safeguarding Authority has also established two new lists of people barred from working with children and vulnerable adults.

Protection of Vulnerable Groups (PVG) Act (Scotland) (2007)

This aims to ensure that those who have regular contact with children and protected adults through paid and unpaid work do not have a known history of harmful behaviour.

Policies and procedures should ensure that once allegations of abuse are reported, suspicions and disclosures of all allegations are responded to consistently and effectively. Policies include the roles and responsibilities at each stage of the process from alerting, reporting through to investigation and outcome. Staff have a duty to report their concerns and it may be that they have seen or heard something that causes concern or that someone has disclosed something to them. Staff do not need proof or evidence before passing on concerns, nor do they need to believe that abuse has occurred in order to start recording behavioural patterns and other indicators. *It Could Never Happen Here* (Churchill *et al*, 1996) offered the following dos and don'ts when hearing a possible disclosure of abuse.

'Do…
- Believe the person
- Stay calm
- Listen patiently
- Let them take their time
- Reassure them that they are doing the right thing in telling you
- Explain to them what you are going to do now
- Write down what they have told you as soon as you can, using their own words as far as possible

Don't…
- Appear shocked, horrified, disgusted or angry
- Make comments or judgments, other than to show sympathy or concern
- Ask leading questions
- Promise to keep secrets
- Give sweeping reassurances
- Remove items that could be evidence
- Confront the alleged abuser'

Once reported, decisions should be taken by managers and others dealing with allegations of abuse about whether an investigation is required. If referral to the police is deemed appropriate then a joint investigation with the police will be carried out, whether the alleged victim is a child or a vulnerable adult, and

if necessary an internal disciplinary will follow. Reference should always be made to local policy and procedures before taking action.

Belle case study part 3

An investigation followed and the police were involved. It transpired that Belle had been sexually abused by her mother's new partner on her occasional visits home. She had clearly been frightened every Friday about the possibility of going home and only reacted on Mondays if she had been at home. Excellent record keeping at the school had made the difference between the situation continuing and being able to uncover the abuse, to stop it and offer Belle the support she needed.

Access to justice

Speaking Up For Justice (1998) and *Achieving Best Evidence* (2000 & 2007) looked closely at the requirements of children and vulnerable adults in the criminal justice system in recognition that there were many barriers to them getting access to justice and a fair trial. New measures were introduced including access to intermediaries, video links and the wider use of communication aids. The Witness Intermediary Scheme is working to ensure that the most vulnerable in our society, including people with learning disabilities, get access to justice and it has already supported many vulnerable witnesses, many of whom would otherwise never have got to court.

These, along with training of professionals in the criminal justice system, aimed at raising their awareness of the needs of alleged victims with learning disabilities has gone some way to improve access. However many critics would say that progress has been slow and that while so many of the people with learning disabilities are not considered able to either manage a police investigation or to participate in the court process, they remain as vulnerable as ever. Perpetrators will continue to target children and adults with learning disabilities, knowing that it is unlikely that they will be caught or charged, let alone convicted within the criminal justice system, and therefore remains an area in which further progress still needs to be made.

New risks

A number of recent pieces of work have identified new areas of risk of sexual abuse of both children and adults with learning disabilities.

The Foreign Office's Forced Marriage Unit collaborated with the Ann Craft Trust and the Judith Trust to look at issues of forced marriage of children and young people with learning disabilities. This is in recognition of the growing evidence of the threat posed by forced marriage to the well-being of both men and women with learning disabilities. Of the 400 cases of forced marriage referred to in the Foreign Office Forced Marriage Unit in 2007, approximately 80 involved people with a learning disability. The expectation that the marriage will be consummated and the result of the couple having children can mean that people with learning disabilities forced into marriage may be subjected to sexual assault and rape. A spouse may have little understanding of learning disabilities and how they might support the person they have married and feelings of resentment and confusion may lead to domestic violence and abuse.

A second area of growing concern is the risks posed by internet sites including dating and friendship sites. While, for some, these sites can undoubtedly offer positive opportunities for building relationships, it is also important that people with learning disabilities are supported to understand the potential risks. A report by Barnardos (2009) highlights a number of dangers faced by children and young people in the age of the computer and the internet including privacy and protection, the security of data and the ever increasing market for child pornography which can also be applied to adults with learning disabilities.

Supporting people with learning disabilities who have been abused

Men and women with learning disabilities who are victims of abuse are not different in relation to the support that they may require. Previous assumptions that the harm inflicted is somehow less, that they will recover more quickly because they have less recall and that they cannot because of their limited intellectual abilities benefit from counselling and therapy have all now been challenged (Cooke, 2000; Fyson, 2005). The problem of accessing appropriate support often lies with post-abuse support services that are unable to adapt to meet the specific needs of people with learning disabilities. Consequently, the support offered may be from learning disability

services without the experience required to assist victims of abuse or from specialist services without reference to the specific needs of the individual (including communication and capacity). There are, however, a limited number of specialist services nationally and they serve as useful contacts for signposting to appropriate support. For example, Respond, a registered charity based in London, offers specialist therapeutic interventions for victims and perpetrators with learning disabilities and together with the Ann Craft Trust have a useful database of counsellors and therapists who work with men and women with learning disabilities nationally.

Conclusion

This chapter has looked at a number of issues relating to the sexual abuse of people with a learning disability such as what is abuse, how to identify any concerns about abuse, what action to take if there are concerns. All services need to consider safeguarding strategies that reduce risk, including safeguards in staff recruitment and staff supervision, creating open cultures, supportive whistle-blowing policies and effective professional development programmes. It is important to ensure that policy, procedure and practice in relation to all issues concerning the sexual abuse of children and adults with learning disabilities are reinforced through regular staff training. Moreover, all policies and safeguarding strategies should be accessible not only to staff and family carers but as much as possible to people with learning disabilities so they are empowered to protect themselves from harm.

References

Ann Craft Trust & ARC (1996) (Revised edition) *It Could Never Happen Here*. London: Department of Health.

Brown H & Craft A (1992) *Working with the Unthinkable: A trainer's manual on the sexual abuse of adults with learning disabilities*. London: FPA.

Brown H, Stein J & Turk V (1995) The sexual abuse of adults with learning disabilities: report of a second two-year incidence survey. *Mental Handicap Research* 8 3–24.

Churchill J, Holding A & Horrocks C (Eds) (1996) *It Could Never Happen Here (Revised Edition)*. Chesterfield and Nottingham: ARC and NAPSAC.

Cooke P (2000) *Disabled Children and Abuse*. Nottingham: Ann Craft Trust.

Craft A (1987) *Mental Handicap and Sexuality*. Tunbridge Wells: Costello.

Department of Children, Schools and Families (2010) *Working Together to Safeguard Children: A guide to inter-agency working to safeguard and promote the welfare of children*. HM Government: DCSF.

Department of Health & Home Office (2000) *No Secrets: Guidance on developing and implementing multi-agency policies and procedures to protect vulnerable adults from abuse*. London: DH.

Fyson R (2005) *Young People with Learning Disabilities who Show Sexually Inappropriate or Abusive Behaviours*. Nottingham: Ann Craft Trust.

Home Office (1998) *Speaking Up For Justice. Report of the interdepartmental working group on the treatment of vulnerable or intimidated witnesses in the criminal justice system*. London: Home Office.

McKenna P (2009) *Three Hazards – Child Protection in the Electronic Age*. London: Barnardos.

Local Authority X v MM and KM [2007] EWHC 2689 (16 November 2007)

Office for Criminal Justice Reform (2000) *Achieving Best Evidence in Criminal Proceedings: Guidance for vulnerable or intimidated witnesses, including children*. London: Home Office.

Office for Criminal Justice Reform (2007) *Achieving Best Evidence in Criminal Proceedings: Guidance for vulnerable or intimidated witnesses, and using special measures*. London: Office for Criminal Justice Reform.

Thesite.org (2010) [online]. Available at: http://www.askthesite.co.uk/homelawandmoney/law/yourrights/sexualoffencesexplained (accessed August 2010).

Turk V & Brown H (1993) The Sexual Abuse of Adults with Learning Disabilities: Results of a two year incidence survey. *Mental Handicap Research* **6** (3) 193–216.

Further reading

ENABLE Scotland (2010) *Sexual Abuse and Learning Disabilities Pack* [online]. Available on: http://www.enable.org.uk/info.php?sid=18&ssid=251.

FPA (2009) *Learning Disabilities Sex and the Law: A practical guide*. England: FPA.

Fyson R & Cromby J (2010) *Memory, sexual abuse and the politics of learning disability*. In: J Haaken & P Reavey *Memory Matters: Contexts for Understanding Sexual Abuse Recollections*. Hove: Routledge.

Hollins S & Sinason V (2005) *Jenny Speaks Out (Books Beyond Words)*. London: Royal College of Psychiatrists.

McCarthy M (1999) *Sexuality and Women with Learning Disabilities*. London: Jessica Kingsley Publishers.

O'Callaghan AC, Murphy G & Clare ICH (2003) The impact of abuse on men and women with severe learning disabilities and their families. *British Journal of Learning Disabilities* **31** (4) 175–180.

Sinason V (2002) Treating people with learning disabilities after physical or sexual abuse. *Advances in Psychiatric Treatment* **8** 424–431.

Chapter 9

Unacceptable sexual behaviour

David Thompson

Introduction

This chapter gives some suggestions on understanding and responding to unacceptable and abusive sexual behaviour. It talks about the behaviour of men and boys with learning disabilities who are more likely to present challenges in this area than women and girls with learning disabilities. However, the ideas given may be helpful when responding to females. Only a very small number of people with learning disabilities have unacceptable or abusive sexual behaviour. Amongst those who do not, all of the issues described below will be relevant.

The information is largely drawn from the author's direct work and research involving men with learning disabilities and their carers. This work sought to provide considered and fair responses to the men's behaviour (see Thompson & Brown, 2007 for more detailed information).

What is unacceptable or abusive sexual behaviour?

What is unacceptable sexual behaviour for some people can be seen as positive by others. Cultural values and religion make it hard to agree on what is acceptable and what is not. On top of this, it is not unusual for any sexual expression shown by people with learning disabilities to be seen as a problem. Rarely is it celebrated as a normal aspect of development.

Here the term unacceptable sexual behaviour is used to cover any sexual behaviour that is imposed on other people without their consent. This includes exposure or sexual touching involving other people with learning disabilities, carers or members of the general public. It does not depend on the intention of the man with learning disabilities, for example, a man with learning disabilities exposing his penis in public is unacceptable whether or not he intends to offend those people who see it, and whether or not he understands about privacy.

Abusive sexual behaviour is any unacceptable sexual behaviour where either the man with learning disabilities intends to sexually abuse another person, or they experience it as abusive. For example, a man with learning disabilities might grab the breast of a female staff member without understanding that this is sexual abuse as the woman does not consent. His lack of understanding does not prevent the woman feeling abused by his sexual behaviour.

Being clear about what is unacceptable or abusive sexual behaviour is the starting point to developing clear responses which might address the man's behaviour. Not doing so runs the risk of tolerating and even encouraging the behaviour. For example, too often some adult men with learning disabilities are allowed to very intimately cuddle adult women in a way that would not be tolerated if the man did not have learning disabilities.

Taking action in the man's best interests

A starting point for any work for men with learning disabilities with unacceptable or abusive sexual behaviour is to assess whether the man has mental capacity to take responsibility for his behaviour i.e. does he understand the unacceptability of his behaviour, the impact it might have on other people and the potential consequence for him? Where the man does have this understanding, it is important not to shield him from the potential consequences. These might be action taken by the police, eviction from a shared service or exclusion from a day opportunities programme.

If the man does lack understanding, the Mental Capacity Act (2005) in England and Wales allows action to be taken in *his* best interests. For some, this will mean putting restrictions on his access to other people. This might include having all male staff, increased levels of supervision, or moving him so

he is no longer living with very vulnerable people. It could also involve giving the man a meaningful consequence to his behaviour. This could be taking away a valued opportunity such as a planned trip with the intention of helping the man understand the seriousness of the behaviour.

It can be argued that taking action when the man does not have capacity to take responsibility for his behaviour is in his best interests because it can protect him from what might happen if his behaviour continues. For example, if public masturbation is not addressed, the man's opportunities to go out may be very restricted, or if sexually touching other people in a day centre is not stopped, the man may need to be (and probably should be) excluded indefinitely from the service.

When making a decision in a man's best interests the Mental Capacity Act requires the following:

▶ the man's views are taken into account

▶ the right people are consulted, including those people who know him best. In most cases this would include the man's family

▶ effort is made to minimise the restrictions placed on the man.

Sometimes very significant restrictions may be suggested. For example, where there is a risk of sexual abuse directed at members of the general public, it may be necessary for the man to only go out with supervision to reduce the risks. Where this happens there needs to be a check as to whether this would be a deprivation of the man's liberty (for which there is protection under Article 5 of the European Convention on Human Rights). In England and Wales, this may require an order from the Court of Protection or a standard authorisation under the Deprivation of Liberty Safeguards (DH, 2008).

Masturbating publically

Chapter 2 sets out some of the common difficulties men with learning disabilities may experience masturbating. Sometimes these concerns are about men or boys with learning disabilities masturbating or trying to masturbate in places where this is visible to other people. There is often a too much acceptance of this behaviour, particularly when this is done in front of other people with learning disabilities or carers. There is usually much greater concern if the men masturbate in front of people in the general public

Chapter 9 – Unacceptable sexual behaviour

including children. The message behind this difference is that people with learning disabilities and their staff do not deserve the same level of respect that other people do. Some men with learning disabilities learn this difference, especially when the consequences to them of masturbating in front of people in the general public are greater.

A challenge with some men with learning disabilities when addressing public masturbation is that they believe that masturbation is wrong wherever it is done. Has anyone told them it is a good and normal thing to do, and where the good places are to do it? This is an important part of sex education for these men. Once it is known that it is OK to masturbate in private, it is easier to be very assertive about public masturbation.

The ways a man is helped to understand where it is OK and not OK to masturbate very much depends on their communication skills. With more able men it is possible to use words to name good places and good times. Some men may benefit from line drawings while with others it will require physically prompting them to go to a private place when they start masturbating.

More able men with learning disabilities when asked about masturbating generally feel bad about it and do not think that men without learning disabilities do it. To make men feel less guilty (about what may be their only sexual experiences), it is good to find ways to help them understand it is normal and healthy. One of the most powerful ways to get this message across is for valued men in their life to say they themselves masturbate.

Day centres and schools often say that these are places where people should not masturbate – even in private and during breaks. Responses should be realistic (some individuals will not cope with not being able to masturbate for prolonged periods) and fair (there is little to stop staff masturbating in their breaks). Rather than constantly trying to stop a man masturbating publicly (and so exposing themselves inappropriately to other people) it can be more effective to give the man some private time.

When men with learning disabilities masturbate in public there are often patterns. Some men do it when other activities offer little interest. For example, a man may not masturbate on a bus, but often does it in specific sessions at the day centre. This can show that the men are making some choices about when they masturbate and so it is more hopeful that it will be possible to put boundaries on time and place.

When men have an understanding of privacy and are choosing to continue to masturbate in public, it is important to treat the behaviour as abusive.

Unacceptable sexual touching

Some men with learning disabilities touch other people sexually without consent. This includes grabbing sexual parts of the body, or rubbing themselves against the person sexually. Typically this involves women with learning disabilities, women staff, and women and children in the general public. Like masturbation in public, this behaviour tends only to be taken seriously when women and children in the general public are involved. Women and men with learning disabilities are wrongly expected to tolerate it, and women staff often feel they have to put up with it as part of the job. This behaviour is sexual abuse in law but the legal system tends to disregard this unless children are the victims.

As stated above, there needs to be clarity as to whether the man has the mental capacity to take full responsibility for his behaviour. It is often the case that men with learning disabilities have some understanding that this behaviour is wrong, but fail to understand the seriousness of it. Many men with learning disabilities learn it is not serious because there are minimal, inconsistent or no consequences to their behaviour.

Work with men should try to help them understand the seriousness of their behaviour. For many this will mean ensuring there are consequences which protect their best interests. If the police are not involved or take no action because of the man's learning disability, then there are grounds to impose consequences which are meaningful to the man. The alternative position of doing nothing risks teaching the men that what they are doing is OK. It can leave them unprepared for the consequences of touching someone who reasonably demands severe action.

In addition to trying to communicate the seriousness of their unacceptable or abusive sexual behaviour and what will happen if they do it again, ideally the men should be helped to understand the impact of their behaviour on their victims. However, empathy – to think about how someone else might feel – is a difficult concept for some men with learning disabilities.

Case study

Robert is a 25-year-old man with learning disabilities who attends a mixed college three mornings a week and he travels to college on public transport. He is very sociable and has a lot of contact with the other students. He is particularly interested in talking to female students and is known for frequently seeking hugs and kisses from them. Some women go out of their way to avoid him because of his behaviour, while others think he is quite funny and humour his suggestion that they are his girlfriends. Some of the female students with learning disabilities are also a target for this behaviour. They find it harder to deal with his attempts at intimate contact and not infrequently are on the receiving end of having their bottoms or breasts grabbed. Staff have inconsistently responded to incidents which they have either witnessed or where women have complained. Usually this is to tell Robert that he can't touch people who don't want it.

This case study shows how often men with learning disabilities learn that they can get away with sexual behaviour, which would not be tolerated if other men do it. It also shows how commonly people with learning disabilities are placed in unacceptably vulnerable situations. Although individual women and the staff are intermittently discouraging Robert's behaviour, he is also getting messages from some woman that it is fine. His behaviour is probably also reinforced by the sexual pleasure he enjoys from the intimate contact.

If work with Robert shows that he lacks capacity to take full responsibility for his unacceptable and abusive sexual behaviour, decisions need to be taken in his best interests. It would be helpful to inform the women that by not responding to Robert's behaviour in a similar way as they would to other men, they are causing greater harm in the long run and they should be encouraged to report any unacceptable sexual behaviour. A meaningful consequence for Robert may be to suspend him from college if he touches anyone without their consent. Explaining to him that this will happen during one-to-one work should help him develop a better understanding of the seriousness of his behaviour. Attention should also be given to involving the police in any future incidents.

Sexual contact with other people with learning disabilities

Attitudes to men with learning disabilities having any sexual contact with other people with learning disabilities vary widely. Some people will stop any sexual contact regardless of the context, others will see it very positively without checking that both parties are consenting. People also respond very differently depending on whether the contact is with another man or a woman, and this can make it very difficult for men to understand what is and is not acceptable.

The focus of responses and support should be on the consent of the people involved – whether this is for hand holding, cuddling or more intimate sexual contact. Different sexual contacts require different levels of understanding. So some people with learning disabilities may be able to consent to hugging (with no physical risks) but not intimate sexual acts (which can have physical risks that the person may not be able to understand even with support).

When trying to establish the relative consent of the people involved, it is useful to consider the following.

▶ Who initiates the contact?

▶ The relative degrees of learning disability. Where there is a significant difference it is extremely unlikely that the less able person will be able to make choices.

▶ Whether both people have the skills and power to say no?

▶ Is one person being tricked into having the sexual contact? For example, the man might say he is a woman's boyfriend, promise to get married or buy her a present when he has no intention of doing so.

Care must be taken not to set too high a demand on the understanding of the people involved. Many services are more comfortable deciding that intimate contact between people with learning disabilities is unacceptable than acceptable. A risk is that people with learning disabilities will learn that they will get into trouble for any sexual contact, which will undermine a good understanding of consent. In response, people with learning disabilities learn to be secretive about sex (which is very different to being private) which enhances their vulnerability to abuse. Where people have the capacity to consent to sexual relationships it is important to support and value sexual opportunities. This could include ensuring that adults have double beds and not putting unnecessary obstacles in people's way to have overnight guests.

Chapter 9 – Unacceptable sexual behaviour

If the decision is that one person lacks capacity to consent to the contact then the strategy needs to ensure that the touching or sex does not continue. As above, work needs to focus on consequences for the man with learning disabilities whose sexual behaviour is unacceptable and other risk reduction methods are in place. Attention also needs to be given to the person on the receiving end of the unacceptable sexual behaviour who may be unhappy about the restrictions placed on contact. This work should take place in the context of child or adult protection policy and procedures.

Less able people with learning disabilities are particularly vulnerable, so advice is to err on the side of caution when consent is in doubt. Sometimes it will be necessary for those involved in the individuals' support to draw clear boundaries about what touch is and is not acceptable and to intervene where necessary. For example, to accept two individuals with severe learning disabilities holding hands but not to sit on each other's laps.

Pornography and other sexual stimuli

Sex has several dimensions for men. First, there is the physical side of rubbing the penis or other sensitive parts of the body. Second, there may be an emotional aspect to the relationship with another person involved, and third, there may also be sexual fantasy involved, for example through the use of pornography. There is some evidence that suggests fantasy plays a smaller part in the sexual lives of men with learning disabilities compared to other men. This is not surprising as fantasy is a cognitive activity. That said, some men with learning disabilities are interested in pornography although their access to this may however be very limited (for example because of the difficulties of buying this independently). They may however have access to other arousing images which are more easily available, for example, holiday brochures or TV magazines.

It is often suggested that men with learning disabilities who have problematic sexual behaviour should be supported to access pornography including videos in theory to 'relieve sexual frustration', although there is no clear evidence to suggest this is helpful. Indeed there are risks, including the idea that other people are sexual objects. However, it also seems unfair to deny men with learning disability access to pornography when other men use it so much. One possible line to draw is accepting men's private use of such pornographic materials they access independently but not providing them with material.

A very few men with learning disabilities gain enjoyment from either exposing unwilling people to pornography or trying to engage them in inappropriate sexual conversation. It can be difficult for carers to distinguish between a man having legitimate interest in talking about sex and being a victim to what can be sexual harassment. For example, a female staff member may be unclear about how to respond if a man with learning disabilities asks them how people have sex. The first time they may believe they are providing honest sex education. However, if the man keeps on asking the same question it has probably turned into something else. It can be helpful to agree and enforce clear boundaries about when and with whom it is OK for men with learning disabilities to talk about sex, and similarly to put limits on what can be talked about.

Very occasionally men with learning disabilities appear to be aroused by things other than adult women or men. This includes images of children but also could be certain objects or textures. Care needs to be taken in thinking the men's interests are so strange or unusual because men with learning disabilities are less able to keep their interests secret (other men don't, for example, have people checking the contents of their bedrooms). Whatever people think of these varied sexual interests, we know that sexual interests are extremely resistant to change.

The major focus of work in this area should be ensuring the men's interests are not a problem for other people, for example, by ensuring other people are not exposed to their sexual interests. Specialist support should be sought where there is a belief that a man is sexually interested in children.

The possibility of the man having been sexually abused

It is too commonly assumed that if a man with learning disabilities is showing some kind of unacceptable or abusive sexual behaviour that he has been sexually abused. There is very little evidence to suggest that this explains the behaviour of the majority of men with learning disabilities although it may be a factor for some (Thompson, 1997; Lindsay 2002; Gilby *et al*, 1989). Therefore where a man is displaying inappropriate or abusive sexual behaviour it is important to consider whether he has been or is being sexually abused.

A useful question to ask is how has the man learnt about the behaviour he is displaying? Men with learning disabilities have less opportunities and ability

to learn about sex than most other people. They may be more dependant on learning from experience. The question being is he doing this because it has happened to him?

Therapy and other treatments

The unacceptable and abusive sexual behaviour of most men with learning disabilities can be managed successfully in local services by providing consistent responses. These should be agreed between family carers, staff and local community learning disability teams. Occasionally more specialist input is necessary, particularly where there are threats, violence or children involved. This may be provided by or accessed via psychology or psychiatry services.

There are a range of different therapeutic approaches taken when working with men who have abusive sexual behaviour. These include psychotherapy and cognitive behavioural work (Cottis, 2008; Murphy et al, 2007). Research looking at those few men with learning disabilities who receive specialist treatment services is at the early stages at identifying what is most effective. However, there are strong indictors of what is minimally required (Lindsay, 2002). This includes not expecting significant risk reduction within two years of therapy. Also the work needs to go beyond sitting in a room talking to the man, to involving and informing those people who support him in his daily life.

Sexual suppressant medication

Sexual suppressant medication may be suggested as a response to unacceptable or abusive sexual behaviour (Cooper, 1995). This should be strongly resisted because of the lack of evidence proving it effective with men with learning disabilities, together with the very worrying side effects profile, for example, growing breasts.

Access to a sexual partner

Another suggestion made when men with learning disabilities have unacceptable or abusive sexual behaviour is that it would not be a problem if the man had a sexual relationship, typically with a woman. This is an unhelpful suggestion largely because there is no evidence that it would work.

There should also be concern about the risks for the sexual partner being sexually exploited by a man with a history of abusive sexual behaviour.

Access to prostitutes may also be suggested but again there is no evidence that this would resolve a man with learning disabilities' unacceptable sexual behaviour. The law is also clear that carers should not support access to any sexual opportunities for people with learning disabilities who are unable to make their own informed choices about this.

Conclusion

Part of understanding the unacceptable or abusive sexual behaviour amongst men with learning disabilities is to think what messages all people with learning disabilities may have received about their sexuality and sexual expression from those who support them. These include the following.

- There are different boundaries of acceptable touch when one person has learning disabilities. For example, many adults are unusually tactile with children and adults with Down's syndrome.
- Masturbation is bad.
- People with learning disabilities are discouraged from having any sexual relationships.
- Unacceptable or abusive sexual behaviour is rarely taken seriously.

This means that a lot of work with men with learning disabilities with unacceptable or abusive sexual behaviour is correcting what has often been unhelpful learning. This work tends only to be seen as important when the men's behaviour becomes a problem. In the interest of men with learning disabilities and those people who might be on the receiving end of their behaviour, more attention should be given to providing all people with learning disabilities with good information about sex.

References

Cooper AJ (1995) Review of the role of antilibidinal drugs in the treatment of sex offenders with mental retardation. *Mental Retardation* **33** 42–48.

Cottis T (Ed) (2008) *Intellectual Disability, Trauma and Psychotherapy*. London: Routledge.

Department of Health (2008) *Mental Capacity Act 2005: Deprivation of liberty safeguards – Code of Practice to supplement the main Mental Capacity Act (2005) Code of Practice*. London: HMSO.

Gilby R, Wolf L & Goldberg B (1989) Mentally retarded adolescent sex offenders: a survey and pilot study. *Canadian Journal of Psychiatry* **34** (6) 542–528.

Lindsay WR (2002) Research and literature on sex offenders with intellectual and development disabilities. *Journal of Intellectual Disability Research* **46** (1) 74–85.

Murphy G, Powell S, Guzman A–M & Hays S (2007) Cognitive-behavioural treatment for men with intellectual disabilities and sexually abusive behaviour: a pilot study. *Journal of Intellectual Disabilities Research* **51** 902–912.

Thompson DJ (1997) Profiling the sexually abusive behaviour of men with intellectual disabilities. *Journal of Applied Research in Intellectual Disabilities* **10** (2) 125–139.

Thompson D & Brown H (2007) *Men with learning disabilities who sexually abuse: Working together to develop response-ability*. Brighton: Pavilion.

Relevant contacts

The Sexuality Support Team, part of Hertfordshire Partnership NHS Foundation Trust, provides advice and training on a wide range of sexual issues for people with learning disabilities.
Tel: 01923 670796
Website: www.hertspartsft.nhs.uk

Respond can provide support for people with learning disabilities who are either the victims or perpetrators of abuse.
Tel: 020 7380 8254
Website: www.respond.org.uk

National Clinical Assessment and Treatment Service, this NSPCC resource provides a national service for children and young people up to the age of 21 where concerns exist about sexually harmful or sexually abusive behaviour.
Tel: 020 7428 1500
Website: www.nspcc.org.uk/freshstart

Chapter 10

Sex education with individuals and in groups

Seema Fitzwater and Jane Noonan

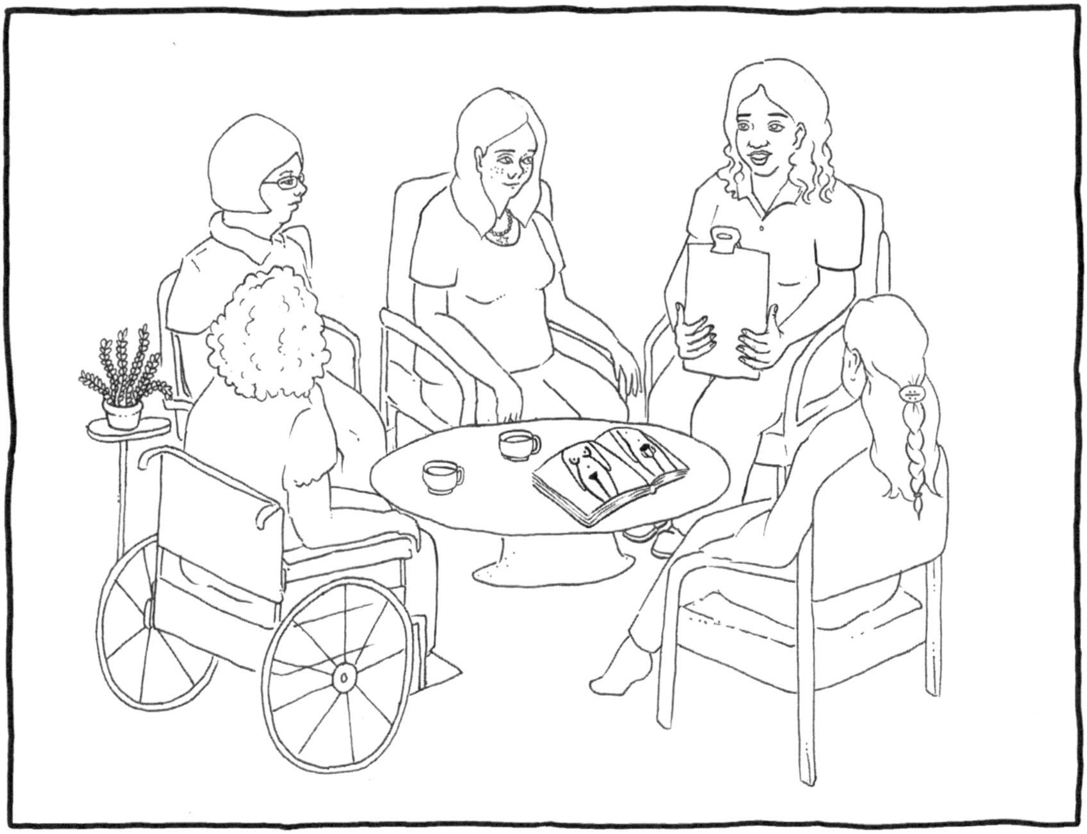

Introduction

This chapter offers guidance on providing sex education. It is based on the direct experiences of the authors who have worked with people with learning disabilities on sexual issues over many years, both individually and in groups. This work has developed by listening to people with learning disabilities talk about their lives. It has also been informed by the views of their families, staff and other professionals.

There are different opinions about sex education and how it should be taught. The approach suggested is to be person centred and respectful of different cultures, sexual orientation, disability, race, age and gender.

The first part of the chapter addresses the following issues:

- the importance of sex education work
- who has responsibility for teaching sex education
- what needs to be taught and where to start
- who, and what, supports the work
- parents' concerns and how they can be supported
- what people with learning disabilities hope for
- choosing resources.

The second part contains a case study which shows what can happen in practice.

The importance of sex education work

Based on the experience of the authors, they have found that sex education work has been effective in helping people with learning disabilities to:

- have a better understanding of their own, and other people's bodies
- know what happens in sex
- develop self-esteem
- understand their rights and responsibilities
- develop strategies to keep themselves safe.

Often this has enabled people with a learning disability to understand what has happened to them and speak out about abuse. The work has also empowered some people to take control of their lives, making decisions around safe sex practices and protection from STIs and pregnancy.

The ability of people with learning disabilities to assert themselves in their sexual relationships is dependent on who they are having sex with. So, for example, a man with mild learning disabilities may be able to make sexual choices when in a relationship with another man with learning disabilities, but could struggle to do so in a sexual relationship with a man without learning disabilities. Similarly women with learning disabilities having sex with men generally find it very difficult to make any choices other than to refuse specific sexual acts. It is very hard for them to get the man to pay any attention to their pleasure. Sex education by itself is unlikely to be able to overcome such differences in power and so other forms of support will be necessary.

Who has responsibility for teaching sex education?

The first challenge of teaching sex education to people with learning disabilities is finding someone who is willing to do it. There are relatively few people who have the necessary experience of working with people with learning disabilities and the confidence to talk about sexual issues. Sexual health workers or

counsellors may lack the skills of making information accessible to people with learning disabilities and may be unaware of the context in which their sexual lives are lived. Learning disability professionals may be anxious to discuss sexual matters with the service users they support.

Often people with learning disabilities talk about sex with those people they trust who they see on a regular basis. This includes family members and frontline staff who may feel unequipped to provide support on the issues raised. A good thing about these people being involved is that people with learning disabilities will be more able to ask for help, to talk things over at a time that suits them. This is preferable to being restricted to the times of a scheduled sex education session.

Rarely will the 'ideal' person be available to provide sex education. It is not helpful to those seeking help merely to be given reasons why there is no one suitable. What is needed is to identify who can best do it and how they can be supported, and this could be through supervision or guidance.

A key skill of anyone providing sex education is to be able to recognise the different sexual opportunities (or lack of opportunities) people with learning disabilities have and to be aware of how their own values and beliefs may influence the people they are working with.

What needs to be taught and where to start

Often sex education is provided in response to a specific issue or incident. Alternatively the person with learning disabilities might be asking for specific information. This can help you decide where to start. For example, the need to teach a girl with learning disabilities about menstruation may have been prompted by her parents discovering that she has started her periods (though ideally support should have been provided before this time).

When sex education is not given in response to a situation, it can be harder to decide what it should cover. It is good to think about what individuals need to know, based on their age, level of learning disabilities and life opportunities. This may cover:

- sexual parts of the body
- masturbation
- privacy
- sex between people of the same and opposite sex
- the possible consequences of sex
- saying yes to wanted touch
- saying no to unwanted touch
- what to do if worried about sexual abuse

It is important to always start by assessing the understanding of the individual and then build the information around this.

One of the most useful things that many people with learning disabilities learn in sex education is that the educator is comfortable talking about sexual issues and will not judge them. This often leads to people with learning disabilities being open about some of the sexual issues and situations they are facing in their own lives. From this the educator is able to tailor their information and support to the individuals' needs.

Who and what supports the work

Staff can feel vulnerable when providing sex education. They may be concerned about what other people will think, including colleagues and family members. It is suggested that people undertaking sex education work make sure the work is supported before they start. This will make them more confident if difficult issues arise during the work.

There are different ways support can be gained. It will depend on who the work is being done with and the content of the work. It is helpful if the organisation has a policy which covers sex education.

It is recommended that some information is given to family members and colleagues before the work starts as a lack of their support could undermine the work. The information could include the skills of the people providing the education, the content of the course, the resources which will be used and what are the limits on confidentiality.

The support of people in daily contact also allows the sex education to be backed up in practical ways, and this may be to reinforce the learning in day-to-day situations. For example, to emphasise the importance of privacy or to be available to talk to a person with learning disabilities about sexual issues outside of the formal sex education.

A minimum requirement is having support from and the supervision of a manager. Particularly if people are new to this work, it is often a good idea for two people to work together.

Parents' concerns and how they can be supported

The parents of people with learning disabilities are often stereotyped as being against their sons and daughters receiving sex education. In reality, this may not be the case and services may use this as an excuse not to support people with learning disabilities with sexual issues. That said, it is not unreasonable for parents to have concerns in this area. The parents of girls and women will often be concerned about their vulnerability to sexual abuse and what would happen if their daughter got pregnant. For parents of boys and men, fears often centre on their son developing unacceptable behaviour.

Providing information to parents about the content of the sex education can address these fears and can also show that the educator has similar concerns. It can also help parents understand that the sex education will be less about teaching people to have sex and more about what is and is not abuse and what to do about it.

Case example
A 10-year-old boy with learning disabilities grabbed a woman's breast whilst with his mother in a supermarket. Her initial reaction was to shout at her son. She was aware that other people were looking, which made her feel uncomfortable, but the mother was worried that her son would grow up to be a sex offender.

Chapter 10 – Sex education with individuals and in groups

The anxiety of the mother in the case example is likely to be huge. Not only may she have to deal with the looks she gets when she's out because her son has learning disabilities, but also because of the impact of his behaviour on other people. The mother may worry that sex education may lead to her son having more ideas about sex and lead to an escalation of his behaviour. It should be clear that a main aim would be to teach him that his behaviour is unacceptable.

Like all parents there may be religious and cultural beliefs which will affect their views about what sex education should and should not be taught. Parents of children with learning disabilities under the age of 16 have rights over their children's involvement in sex education. For older people, parental rights are more limited, but it is still good practice to wherever possible seek support.

Parent groups

Parents of people with learning disabilities can be supported by giving them the opportunity to meet with other parents. This allows them to discuss their hopes and concerns about sex and relationships for their children, to support each other and to gain information. This could be a one-off session or a series of meetings.

The authors ran a group over a number of weeks for mothers of school-age children with learning disabilities from diverse cultural backgrounds. Some of the issues which came up were about supporting their daughters with menstruation. Most mothers only felt comfortable supporting their daughters with sanitary pads. Muslim mothers within the group said their religious beliefs were against the use of tampons. Other mothers were not making tampons available to their daughters because they were either too embarrassed to teach their use, or did not think their daughter would be able to use them. Some mothers were afraid of toxic shock syndrome.

It seemed that the mothers were able to take on board constructive criticism and advice far more readily from each other. Some people within the group did not trust professionals and felt isolated from mothers whose son/daughter did not have a learning disability. They felt that their concerns were different and were more difficult to deal with.

Some of the mothers were still struggling with coming to terms with their children's learning disabilities and life opportunities. They used the group as a rare place where they were able to be open and share their concerns honestly, which some had not previously voiced.

The others gained the confidence to challenge the lack of sex education their children were receiving at school and they were also able to access resources to help them teach sex and relationships at home. Group members also formed lasting contacts and friendships with each other.

What people with learning disabilities hope for

One of the tensions in sex education work is the differences between the hopes of people with learning disabilities and the concerns of families and staff. This theme is explored further in Chapter 6 on supporting relationships. Generally people with learning disabilities are not asking for protection but for the removal of restrictions on their opportunities for relationships. Those people who can voice their desire say they want:

- to have boyfriends or girlfriends
- to get support to meet potential partners
- to be less supervised when with a partner
- to have sex
- to get married
- to have children.

Advice to people doing sex education work is to be honest about the reality of people's lives and the way decisions are often made for them. It can also be helpful to enable people with learning disabilities to find the confidence to challenge some of the restrictions placed on their lives.

Choosing resources

Having access to good resources is essential for conducting sex education work with people who have learning disabilities. At the end of this chapter, there is a list of resources which you may find helpful. When choosing resources, the following should be considered:

- the comprehension skills of the people receiving the education

- whether the resources reflect the likely sexual experiences of people with learning disabilities
- what messages are being given by what is included and what is not, for example, if there are no images of same sex relationships or pictures of women getting pregnant, it suggests these are not acceptable
- conventionally attractive images may make people insecure about their own body images
- representations of different ethnic groups and people with different kinds of disabilities.

Although they may be embarrassing to some, generally sexually explicit resources are required, and this may include line drawings, DVDs and models. People doing sex education work may need time to feel comfortable and confident using such resources.

The opportunities presented by everyday life can also be excellent resources for sex and relationships work, for example, talking about friends or relatives who are getting a divorce or using a storyline in a soap opera about same sex relationships.

Case study

This case study highlights some of the issues that need to be considered when undertaking sex education and the importance of working in partnership with staff and family members.

> Kerry is 22-year-old woman with learning disabilities who lives in a residential care service. In the past Kerry was sexually abused by her stepfather, and although she continues to have a relationship with her mother, she only sees her when she comes to visit Kerry in the care home.
>
> Kerry has a 25-year-old boyfriend called Simon. Simon has had sexual relationships before and lives with his parents and travels to see Kerry. They have been boyfriend and girlfriend for eight months and Kerry has been telling staff she wants to marry Simon.

> Staff at the care home are anxious about Kerry's vulnerability and feel they have a responsibility to closely supervise the couple when they are together in the home to avoid the possibility of sex. Her mother supports this approach, however, both Kerry and her boyfriend are able to go out without staff support and often will do so together. Kerry has not received any sex education since she attended school and staff are uncomfortable to discuss sex with her as they are not sure what to say. When Kerry raises the subject they tend to say that she should wait until she is married. They are also afraid of how talking about sex might bring up Kerry's memories of abuse.

This example is typical of situations where carers will try to stop people with learning disabilities having sex by discouraging it and making sure that it does not happen when they are around. People with learning disabilities learn from this that it is best not to tell carers that they are having sex to avoid 'getting into trouble' – even when they have been sexually abused. It also means that sex, when it does happen, may be in undesirable places like toilets and secluded public places and the sex is likely to be rushed because of the fear of getting caught.

This is the worse possible context for sex to be enjoyable and safe for both people involved. When it involves a man and a woman, the woman with learning disabilities is likely to be more disadvantaged. There is significant risk that hurried penetration will be painful, and aside from pregnancy, the risks of abuse and sexually transmitted diseases are greater for women.

The carers may think that they are acting in Kerry's best interests by supervising her when she is with Simon in the home, but they may instead be taking away her right to make decisions she is able to make herself.

Sex education

The starting point for sex education is to help the staff and Kerry's mother to see that they are taking a 'head in the sand approach' to Kerry's needs. Not talking about it will not make the problem go away and without the support of these people the work can be undermined.

The direction of the work will depend on the support that is available from Kerry's mother and the staff if Kerry is having, or wants to have, a sexual relationship which is consensual. It may be that the only option will be for the work to acknowledge that unfair restrictions on Kerry's personal life are being imposed. This may lead to thinking about how this can be challenged.

Alternatively, it may lead to discussing whether Kerry would be able to have sex with her boyfriend in her bedroom.

Consideration should be given to Simon's potential need for education, and whether those around him would, or would not, support a sexual relationship with Kerry. For example, how would they respond if he spent a night with Kerry? This can raise difficult issues of confidentiality.

Whilst it is likely that Kerry could benefit from formal sex education, for example in a group context, her needs will be better met in the long term if there are people who she sees on a regular basis who she can discuss personal issues with. Some staff may be supportive of talking openly about sex with Kerry, but are nervous of the response of other staff. What often happens is that people with learning disabilities learn with whom it is best to talk about personal issues. A good approach would be to find out from Kerry who she would like to talk to about sex and relationships. This could be her mother or a staff member but it would be inappropriate for a man to do this work alone with Kerry.

Whether the sex education is with an individual with whom Kerry is in regular contact or with a specialist worker, the following would be good practice:

- find a good time and place to talk with which Kerry is comfortable
- try to explain that the discussions will be private, but that action will need to be taken if there is concern of further abuse
- ask Kerry what she would like to learn
- find out what Kerry already knows about relationships and sex; some of this may be wrong and may need to be corrected
- listen and look at body language, assess how comfortable Kerry is and do not talk about things that she is not comfortable with. It may be important to come back to some difficult issues at a later stage
- make sure you understand what Kerry is saying, repeat certain points back and say 'is that what you meant?'
- check Kerry's understanding by allowing her to talk as much as possible. Prompts such as 'what do you think that means?' can be helpful
- use examples when teaching which you know Kerry can relate to. Ask her if she can think of examples

- find out what words Kerry uses for sexual parts of the body and sex
- do not assume words about sex are understood correctly
- think about different communication methods and appropriate resources that may aid understanding
- always be aware of time. Although it may not work well for the person providing the sex education, often people with learning disabilities benefit from short, regular sessions. This can avoid flooding people with too much information at once
- think about Kerry's self-esteem and try to make her feel good about herself.

Possible key messages for the work are given below. They reflect the need to try to make things as simple and clear as possible.

- Women can enjoy masturbation.
- Women can enjoy sex with a man or another woman.
- Sex and other touching is good if both people want it.
- Women and men can do different things when they have sex together.
- You don't have to do things that you don't like with your boyfriend. For example, having his penis in your mouth.
- Penetration of the vagina should feel good. If it doesn't, ask the man to stop.
- You might not want to have sex during a period.
- You can get pregnant if a man puts his penis in your vagina.

Chapter 7 on pregnancy and parenting argues for an honest discussion with women with learning disabilities about pregnancy. Any discussion with Kerry about her wanting to have a baby should be informed by whether there are any physiological reasons why she may not achieve this (for example, women with Down's syndrome have reduced fertility) or the risk of a child being taken into care.

When discussing contraception, while it is good to talk about condoms, it is more realistic to focus on those forms that are not controlled by men. This is because Kerry, as is the case with most women with learning disabilities (and indeed many other women) will be unlikely to be able to insist on their use. Merely discussing contraception will not be enough and it is likely that Kerry may need support to go to a GP or family planning clinic to make this possible.

When sex education is being provided by someone who is not in regular contact with Kerry, it is especially important to talk through who else she could talk to if she has any worries or questions now or in the future.

Conclusion

Sex education does not have to take place in formal sessions. Some of the best work is done informally by those people in day-to-day contact with people with learning disabilities. Family members and carers should be less worried about getting it wrong than leaving people with learning disabilities without good information.

At times there is a place for additional support, and this may be sex education courses or groups run in schools, colleges or other settings. It may also be one-to-one work undertaken in response to a specific need. Ideally people with learning disabilities have access to all these forms of support and education. The value of people with learning disabilities supporting each other should also be recognised and this can happen most obviously in group sessions, but also informally when people have friends that they can confide in.

Work with individuals is rarely effective in isolation. It is often also necessary for carers and staff to be supported to think about how best to support people with learning disabilities with sexual issues.

Finally staff and carers need to accept that people with learning disabilities will make mistakes with relationships and sex. This is not necessarily a problem: everyone should have the opportunity to learn from these common life experiences.

Further resources

CHANGE (2010) [online]. Available at: www.changepeople.co.uk.
Has a set of five booklets on sexuality issues, using pictures and accessible text.

Elfrida Society (2010) *Period Problems: What you can do*. London: Elfrida Society.
Illustrated accessible information on periods.

Elfrida Society (2010) *Your Private Parts.* London: Elfrida Society.
Easy-read pack for women with learning disabilities.

Life Support Productions (2002) [DVD] *Jason's private world.* London: Life Support Productions.
A DVD about men's bodies and masturbation for people with learning disabilities.

Life Support Productions (2002) [DVD] *Kylie's Private World.* London: Life Support Productions.
A DVD about women's bodies and masturbation for people with learning disabilities.

McCarthy M & Millard M (2003) *Supporting Women with Learning Disabilities Through the Menopause.* Brighton: Pavilion Publishing.

McCarthy M & Thompson D (2007) *Sex and the 3Rs.* Brighton: Pavilion Publishing.

Scott L & Kerr-Edwards L (1999) *Talking together … About growing up: A workbook for parents of children with learning disabilities.* London: FPA.

Voice UK (2002) [DVD]. *Assert Yourself.* Derby: Voice UK.
Actors with learning disabilities perform in this training DVD to help people with learning disabilities be more assertive.